Vanguard
Plan and profile, 1946

Battle Honours

Armada	1588
Cadiz	1596
Portland	1653
Gabbard	1653
Scheveningen	1653
Lowerstoft	1665
Four Days' Battle	1666
Orfordness	1666
Barfleur	1692
Louisburg	1758
Quebec	1759
Martinique	1762
Nile	1798
Syria	1840
Jutland	1916

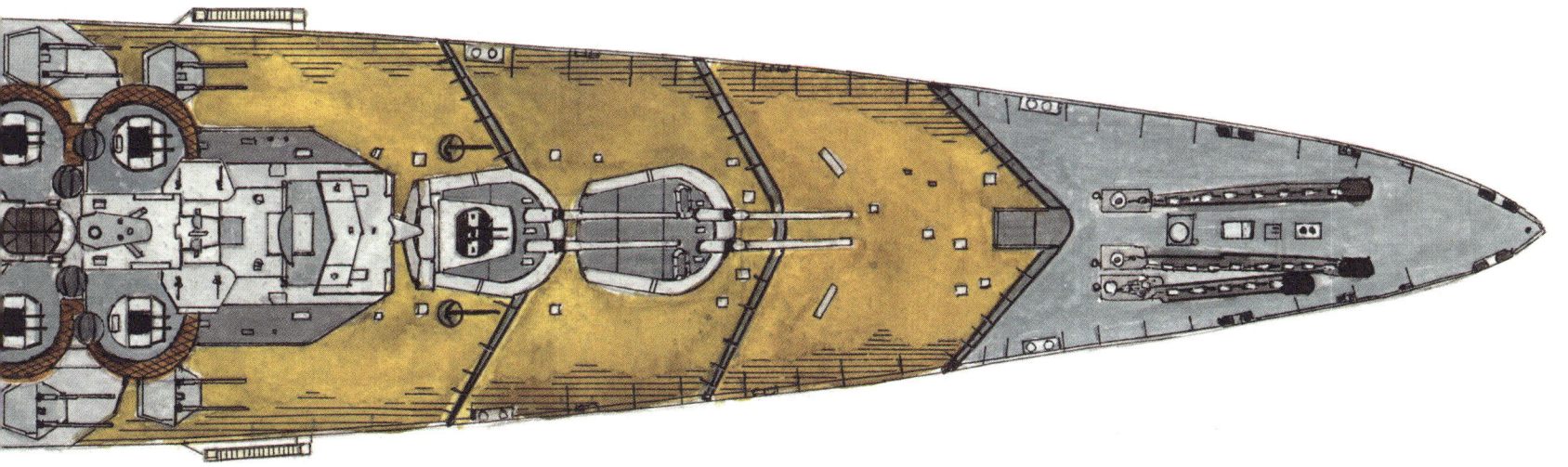

THE LAST BRITISH
BATTLESHIP
HMS VANGUARD 1946–1960

R A BURT

Seaforth
PUBLISHING

Title page: Port quarter view of *Vanguard* in December 1946 on her shakedown cruise to Gibraltar. Note that her radar aerial has been removed from the top of the mainmast and replaced with a short flagpole for the Royal Ensign for the following Royal Tour in February 1947.

In Memory of my brother Kenneth Burt

Copyright © R A Burt 2019

First published in Great Britain in 2019 by
Seaforth Publishing,
A division of Pen & Sword Books Ltd,
47 Church Street,
Barnsley S70 2AS
www.seaforthpublishing.com

Reprinted 2020

British Library Cataloguing in Publication Data
A catalogue record for this book is available from the British Library

   ISBN 978 1 5267 5226 0 (HARDBACK)
   ISBN 978 1 5267 5227 7 (EPUB)
   ISBN 978 1 5267 5258 4 (KINDLE)

All rights reserved. No part of this publication may be reproduced or transmitted in any form or by any means, electronic or mechanical, including photocopying, recording, or any information storage and retrieval system, without prior permission in writing of both the copyright owner and the above publisher.

The right of R A Burt to be identified as the author of this work has been asserted by him in accordance with the Copyright, Designs and Patents Act 1988.

Pen & Sword Books Limited incorporates the imprints of Atlas, Archaeology, Aviation, Discovery, Family History, Fiction, History, Maritime, Military, Military Classics, Politics, Select, Transport, True Crime, Air World, Frontline Publishing, Leo Cooper, Remember When, Seaforth Publishing, The Praetorian Press, Wharncliffe Local History, Wharncliffe Transport, Wharncliffe True Crime and White Owl.

All photographs and line drawings from the author's collection.

Typeset and designed by Stephen Dent
Printed and bound in India by Replika Press Pvt Ltd

Contents

Preface	6
Foreword and Acknowledgements	6
Introduction	7
Design and Construction	14
Launch, 30 November 1944	18
Vanguard: As-Completed Data	34
Hull and Special Features	35
Armament	44
Armour	53
Machinery	54
Bridgework and Funnels	63
Radar Equipment	65
The Royal Tour of 1947	70
Appearance Changes	82
Battleship Design after *Vanguard*	83
Criticism of *Vanguard* and the Demise of the Battleship	91
Appendix A: Service History	110
Appendix B: Comparison with the French *Jean Bart* and the US *Iowa*.	127
Bibliography	128

Preface

The traditions of the Royal Navy are bound up in the histories of its ships. The battles which it has fought and won are incidents in the lives of vessels whose names we know and whose deeds in every century have stirred the nation's blood. Although the materials of which they are built may differ from age to age, the wood and sails of yesterday giving way to the steel, steam, gas turbines and nuclear power of today, when their hulls and cordage become worn out and obsolete they are broken up, or in the kinder, more understanding language of a past age, they are 'taken to pieces'. Their spirit, however, is not destroyed but goes on to be an integral part of the Royal Navy's history and some day later will enter a newly-launched hull which bears the same name and will infuse this new addition to the fleet with all the glory and lustre which it has won in an earlier time.

The Battle Honours will be emblazoned for all to see, an inspiration which none can ignore. Decked out in a new guise and being the latest word in the inventions of its day, each of these magnificent veterans goes into a career extremely confident in its knowledge of the past and the ability to add another laurel to the garlands it has already won

The newest and latest addition to the capital ships programme in 1946 bore the 360-year-old honoured name of *Vanguard*, which reappeared in a time of great unrest, having just seen a World War and about to enter into a so-called Cold War. Great Britain was at a very low ebb and its people hoping for a lasting peace whilst striving to reach some sort of Utopia.

The ninth *Vanguard* of 1946 holds a special place in history, being the last British battleship of the Dreadnought era to be completed and the last of a magnificent type of vessel of which the world will never see again.

HMS *Vanguard* had a lot to live up to and the Royal Navy still had to carry out, albeit in the less arduous conditions of peacetime, its duties of keeping peace and order on the world's oceans which had never been easy during any period in maritime history.

The protection of the sea lanes for the safety and the well-being of them that go down to the sea in ships and that do business in great waters, is a worthy task and one to which the Royal Navy has always proved itself equal by its efficiency, its humanity and above all, its calm and unruffled common sense.

Whatever role the *Vanguard* played during her lifetime she did not fail to do it as nobly as befits a veteran who could boast among her battle honours such glorious names as the Armada, the Nile and Jutland.

Foreword and Acknowledgements

After the completion of *British Battleships 1919-1945* in 1993 I turned my attention to our last and probably finest battleship, HMS *Vanguard*. After studying all the official and relevant material I could find, the manuscript began to take its course. A few drawings were completed and then, along with the partially finished typescript, the material was filed away after about 18 months.

It lay dormant for many years and only just resurfaced at the beginning of 2018 when I was finally encouraged to continue and finish the manuscript. I can offer no real reason or excuse for this rather prolonged hiatus, but with the completion, at last, this publication brings to a close the run of British battleship histories of my previous three books which now cover the period from 1889 to 1960.

During this lengthy period of the project I have had the help from the usual establishments such as the National Maritime Museum, the Imperial War Museum, the British Library, Public Records Office (now The National Archives) the Admiralty Library and many friends who today are sadly no longer with us.

First, I should like to thank the late W P Trotter and T Maskell. Also the late A S Norris and J Hitchon for their help over the years.

Many thanks are extended to J A Roberts who helped with material.

A special thank you must be made to the late T W Ferrers-Walker who encouraged me to complete this book and supplied me with photographs and information on *Vanguard* during the years of the ship's scrapping when he was constantly onboard her. I must also express my gratitude to my publishers Seaforth, with special thanks to Julian Mannering who has made every effort to make the work such a quality production.

Further thanks are extended to A D Mote, S Chumbley and S Dent.

Last but not least, I must give praise to my wife Janice who has, for almost fifty years, put up with my journey into warship studies and has helped all the way through this opus with research, proof reading and typing.

Introduction

To lead into the construction of *Vanguard*, a short résumé is given here into the process of the design of the five *King George V* class battleships of 1936. They had been designed under the severe restrictions of the 1921 Washington Naval Treaty which was further extended by subsequent treaties of 1930 and 1935 in which agreements between Great Britain, France, Russia and the USA had limited standard displacement to 35,000 tons, meaning that any new design would be correspondingly restricted.

From early 1920 through to 1935 Great Britain had conducted extensive tests and put forward numerous designs for new battleship construction and had been correlating information gained from battle experience during the First World War which would be used in any new capital ship design that the Royal Navy would build in the future.

During the early 1930s there was much anxiety over warship construction, with all the major powers eager to begin enhancement of their battle fleets with new additions, especially powerful battleships which was still seen as the backbone of any navy. Although the new treaties of 1935 and 1936 limited capital ship displacement to 35,000 tons and maximum gun calibre to 14in, there was what was called an 'escalator clause' in the fine print of the treaty which meant that these figures could be exceeded if it became known that a non-treaty power was building any ships in excess of this tonnage. In February 1938 the main powers had asked Japan for assurances that it would not exceed the treaty limits and warned that Great Britain and the USA would escalate their own tonnage if no such assurances were given. Japan refused to release any information about their fleet programme, simply pointing out that their fresh construction had no aggressive intent. In the face of such secrecy from a major power, the US Navy insisted an increase in tonnage to 45,000 tons and of gun calibre to 16in. Great Britain, however, had already designed its new class of battleships strictly adhering to the earlier limit of 35,000 tons and armed with 14in guns, and construction of these was to go ahead at the end of treaty restrictions. Requests had been placed with the Director of Naval Construction's (DNC's) department for a suitable battleship layout and as many as twenty such designs were submitted to the Board for approval. The final result was a design designated '14.0' which was considered the most desirable by all concerned including the DNC himself, Sir Arthur John. (The ships were actually built under his successor Sir Stanley Goodall.) On 1 January 1937, when the battleship-building holiday finally came to an end, Britain laid down two battleships of the *King George V* class and a further three in July of the same year.

The features of the design were as follows:

1. The only British battleship to have 14in guns (apart from the ex-Chilean *Canada* taken over in the First World War) and the first to have quadruple turrets.
2. The first to have a dual-purpose secondary armament.
3. The first to be completed with radar.
4. The first to be designed to carry aircraft.
5. The first to be completed without a heavily-armoured conning tower since 1877.

The adoption of the 14in gun had been due to the London Naval Treaty of 1936 which had required a reduction in the maximum permitted gun calibre from 16in to 14in and Great Britain favoured this calibre and based their new design around it. There were many variations put forward for the main-gun layout. Although quadruple mountings were finally agreed on, it was found necessary to reduce one turret to a twin mount to save weight and use the savings to improve magazine protection which was a major feature of the design.

They were the first British battleships to be given dual-purpose secondary guns after lengthy discussions owing to the fact that some favoured separate anti-torpedo and anti-aircraft batteries. The 5.25in gun was finally accepted as a powerful-enough calibre to stop destroyers and anything smaller and the heaviest gun that was capable of being handled with sufficient rapidity to deal with attacking aircraft at long range. (In practice, however, the gun was reported to be too heavy for rapid AA fire, especially when the range closed.) The light AA installation varied, with 32 x 2pdrs (8-barrel mounts) being supplied to the early ships of the class.

The ships completed with a very flush-decked hull with only a slight sheer forward owing to the Admiralty requirement that all turrets forward could fire at 3 degrees depression over all arcs of fire but owing to the lack of freeboard at the bows the ships proved very wet in a seaway and at times this affected the efficiency of the forward turrets.

Compared with *Nelson* and *Rodney* (1927) the design had increased protection against air attack, better distribution of side armour, more efficient sub-division and a much improved system of underwater protection owing to numerous tests carried out on Job 74 before the war. This was a full-size mock-up of a vessel's midships section against which various explosive charges were placed (up to 1,000lb TNT) to ascertain the strength and best form of application for armour plating and bulkheads etc, which

PARTICULARS OF *KING GEORGE V* CLASS AS COMPLETED

	Laid down	Launched	Completed
King George V	1.1.1937	21.2.1939	11.12.1940
Prince of Wales	1.1.1937	3.5.1939	31.3.1941
Duke of York	5.5.1937	28.2.1940	4.11.1941
Anson	22.7.1937	24.2.1940	22.6.1942
Howe	1.6.1937	9.4.1940	29.8.1942

Displacement (tons):
37,754 (light), 41,858 (load), 42,245 (deep).

Dimensions
Length: 700ft (pp), 745ft (oa)
Beam: 103ft
Draught: 28–33ft

Armament
10 x 14in (80rpg)
16 x 5.25in
32 x 2pdr

Armour
Main belt 15–14in
Bulkheads 12–10in
Turrets 13–7in
Deck 5–6in
Conning tower 3–5in

Machinery
Parsons turbines driving 4 screws.
110,000shp for 28 knots
Fuel: 3,770 tons.

Complement
1,400 average.

Right: After a very busy war, having served in both the Home and Pacific Fleets, HMS *King George V* enters Portsmouth harbour on 6 March 1946 showing her general layout and final configuration. Note the barrier on the deck amidships added after the catapult and aircraft equipment had been removed.

could then be given to new battleship construction. The flat armoured deck of *Nelson* was retained and placed one deck higher but her internal side belt was dropped in favour of a flat external belt, the necessity of this being demonstrated during pre-war firing tests against the German battleship *Baden* in 1921 and further tests against HMS *Superb* and *Emperor of India*. The massive bridge tower and general layout of the aircraft hangar and superstructure etc followed the pattern adopted for the reconstructed *Warspite*, *Valiant* and *Queen Elizabeth* but with the addition of a second funnel.

In 1943 a report was drawn up by Captain Oliver Bellasis after a visit to the USA comparing *King George V* to the battleship *Washington* (a US treaty restricted design). It makes interesting reading:

> The turrets are more heavily protected than ours but arrangements for handling shells are simplified to a degree which would not be acceptable in HM ships. The 5in turrets are understood to be much lighter than our 5.25in mountings and much closer together. There are objections to the latter feature on the score of possible damage. Compared with *King George V Washington* has a much smaller armoured freeboard, an inferior armoured deck and a soft forward end. In *KGV* the conning tower has much lighter armour but in the aggregate the protected space in *KGV* is much more than in the US ship and the protection is better. Torpedo damage to the *North Carolina* has revealed a weakness compared to *KGV* viz – greater chance of flooding over third deck (corresponding to middle deck on *KGV* due to its position lower in the ship). *Washington* has a treble bottom, which, however, does not give any appreciable advantage over a double bottom of comparable weight and depth – later US ships reverted to a double bottom. The metacentric height is only slightly greater than *KGV* in spite of the larger beam, probably due to the massive superstructure and

14in GUNS AS MOUNTED IN THE *KING GEORGE V* CLASS

Mk III Mounting Weights
Four guns and mechanism	370 tons
Four balance weights	395 tons
Total weight of mounting	1,582 tons

Mk II Mounting Weights
Two guns and mechanism	185 tons
Two balance weights	23 tons
Total weight of mounting	915 tons
Weight of shell	1,590lbs
Weight of charge	338lbs
Elevation of gun	40 degrees
Depression of gun	3 degrees
Distance between guns	8ft
Muzzle velocity	2,475ft/tons

heavy conning tower. The riddled stability would be poor compared to *KGV* because of her soft ends. *Washington* had considerable trouble with vibration when first commissioned and improvements have been obtained at the expense of some additional weight and interchange of propellers. It is understood that the condition is still not good. The size of the US expansion is remarkable and it appeared to me that there is no doubt that America really intends to have a navy. To our standards at any rate it seems rather too little thought and discussion has been given to the characteristics of the ship, yet the ships seem remarkably, almost disturbingly good – on paper at any rate.

In service throughout the Second World War, the *King George V* class proved their worth many times. They were good 35,000-ton ships but like all treaty-restricted ships they obviously could have been so much better without the limitations imposed upon their size and armament. (For more information on the *King George V* class see *British Battleships 1919–1945*.)

The design of the turrets was based on the well-tried principles of the earlier 13.5in and 15in mountings with the ammunition being supplied in three stages. The magazines were positioned below the shell rooms, which in turn caused some problems in the design of the central gun-loading hoists. The method of loading the shell into the trunk was completely redesigned to provide a live shell ring holding four shells per gun. A fixed loading angle was adopted for simplicity of handling. A great deal of attention was paid to flash-tightness which resulted in the mountings being mechanically more complex but early trials proved successful and the mountings were therefore adopted for the new battleship design of 1936.

Further Capital Ship Construction

After the completion of the design for the five *King George V*s and with their construction underway in 1937, further battleship development continued to be studied in great detail. In the face of constant agitation regarding fresh building plans from abroad (Germany, Italy and especially Japan) the situation for Great Britain was proving to be one of great concern. Although naval treaties limiting fresh construction were still in place at the time, it could not be guaranteed that the major powers would heed to the written word. By the start of 1937 the Royal Navy still possessed twelve battleships and three battlecruisers (fifteen capital ships) but although many of them had undergone some degree of modernisation, apart from *Nelson* and *Rodney*, they had all been constructed during the First World War.

A need to update the battle fleet was viewed by the Admiralty as very necessary but there were misgivings about the size of ships that were required for any modern warfare. There was the school of thought that wanted very large, powerful battleships armed with the biggest guns possible and on the other hand, there were those who suggested a smaller, more compact battleship with guns no larger than those that had been given to the new *King George V*s (14in). Looking abroad it was seen that the US Navy were planning ships with 16in guns, there were hints from France, Germany and Italy suggested that any new ships would carry guns of 15in calibre, and there was great secrecy from Japan over just what kind of capital ships they might build and what calibre they would carry. This was all extremely worrying. On 8 January 1938 the Admiralty made its concerns known:

> The question of the size of gun to be carried by capital ships now appears to be settled as the Japanese refused to accept the 14in gun and the size of future ships built in other countries than Japan is thereby raised to 16in. It is the view of the

King George V General Profile as Fitted, 1940

1. 'X'+'Y' engine rooms.
2. 'X'+'Y' boiler rooms.
3. 'A'+'B' engine rooms.
4. 'A'+'B' boiler rooms.

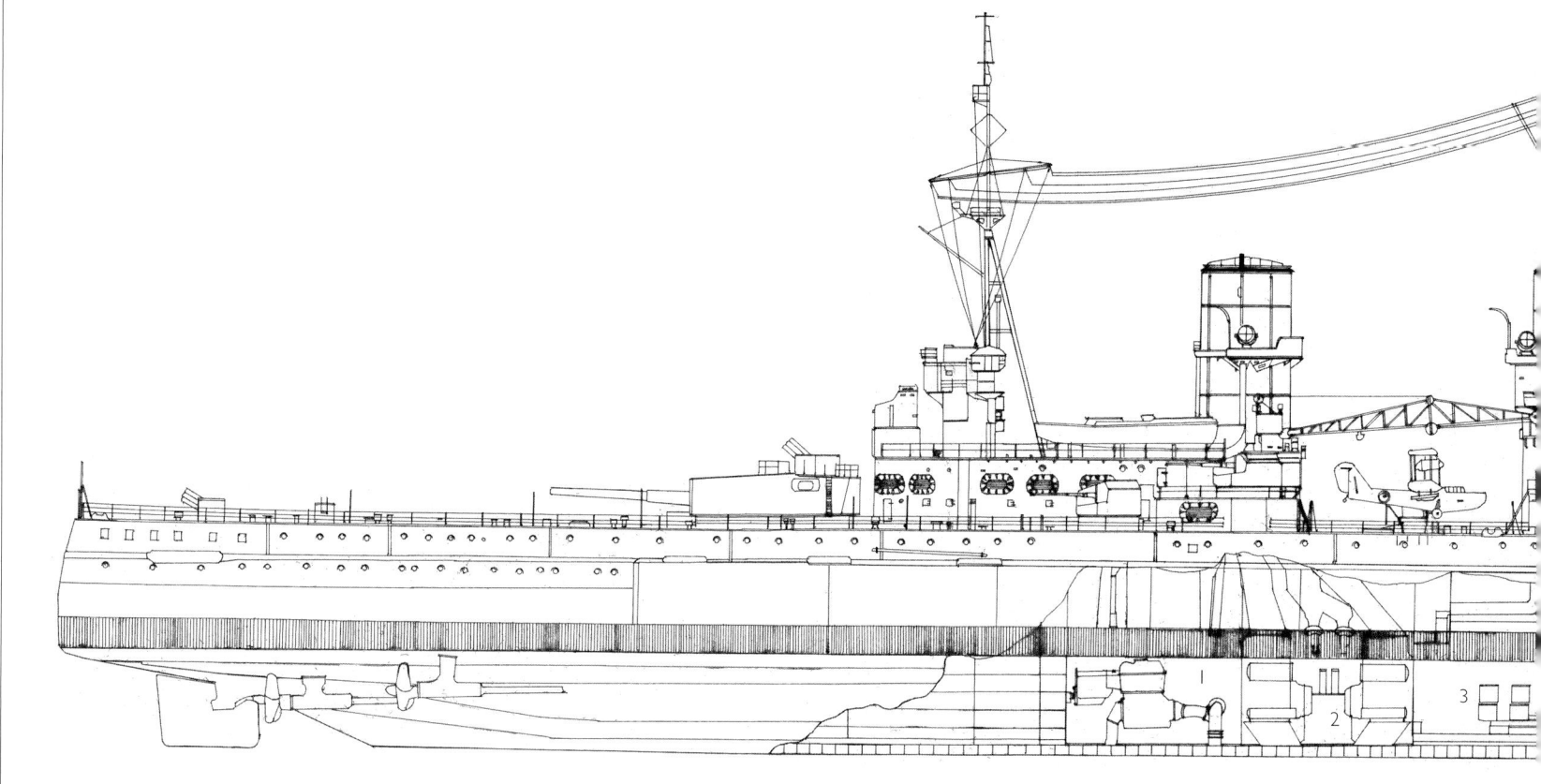

LEGEND OF PARTICULARS FOR PROPOSED NEW BATTLESHIPS FOLLOWING *KING GEORGE V* CLASS, 1938 (*LION CLASS*)

	KGV	'16a-38'	'16B-38'	'14a-38'
Displacement:	35,000 tons	35,000 tons	35,000 tons	35,000 tons
Length:	740ft wl	740ft wl	740ft wl	740ft wl
Beam:	103ft	103ft	103ft	103ft
Draught:	28ft	28ft	28ft	28ft
SHP:	110,000	96,000	110,000	110,000
Speed:	28 knots	28 knots	28½ knots	28½ knots
Main armament:	10 × 14in	9 × 16in	9 × 16in	12 × 14in
Secondary armament:	16 × 5.25in	12 × 5.25in	12 × 5.25in	12 × 5.25in
AA guns:	4 × 2pdr	4 × 2pdr	4 × 2pdr	4 × 2pdr
	4 × MGs	4x MGs	4 × MGs	4 × MGs

Armour protection was the same in all designs, being a 15in thick main belt reducing to 5½in at the bottom edge, 14–4½in over machinery, turrets 13–9–7in and decks 5–5½in and 6in over magazines.

Weights:
Hull	13,215 tons	13,220 tons	13,220 tons	13,200 tons
Armour	12,500 tons	12,160 tons	12,160 tons	12,180 tons
Armament	6,050 tons	6,560 tons	6,560 tons	6,450 tons
Machinery	2,685 tons	2,550 tons	2,650 tons	2,650 tons
General equipment	1,050 tons	1,050 tons	1,050 tons	1,050 tons

Admiralty that the Japanese would be faced with grave difficulty if they exceed this calibre of 16in. The various reports that have been received lead to the conclusion that Japan probably intends to build ships carrying 16in guns of a size of 42,000 or 43,000 tons. It would clearly be a disadvantage that we should continue to build 35,000-ton ships to match larger ships which may be built by Japan. The Admiralty are consequently of the opinion that it is desirable to take some steps now.

In March 1938 the following statement was issued:

In view of reports of Japanese naval construction not in conformity with limits of the London Naval Treaty of 1936 and of failure of Japanese Government to furnish satisfactory assurances in the matter, it has been decided that the United Kingdom and United States Government will exercise their right under Article 25 of the treaty to depart from treaty limitations in respect of the upper limits of capital ships.

Plans were therefore put forward by the Admiralty to lay down and construct a new class of battleship which could possibly be armed with 16in guns. It was only natural that the design would follow closely that of the *King George V*s but with certain naval treaties still in force and Great Britain adhering to them, it proved

INTRODUCTION

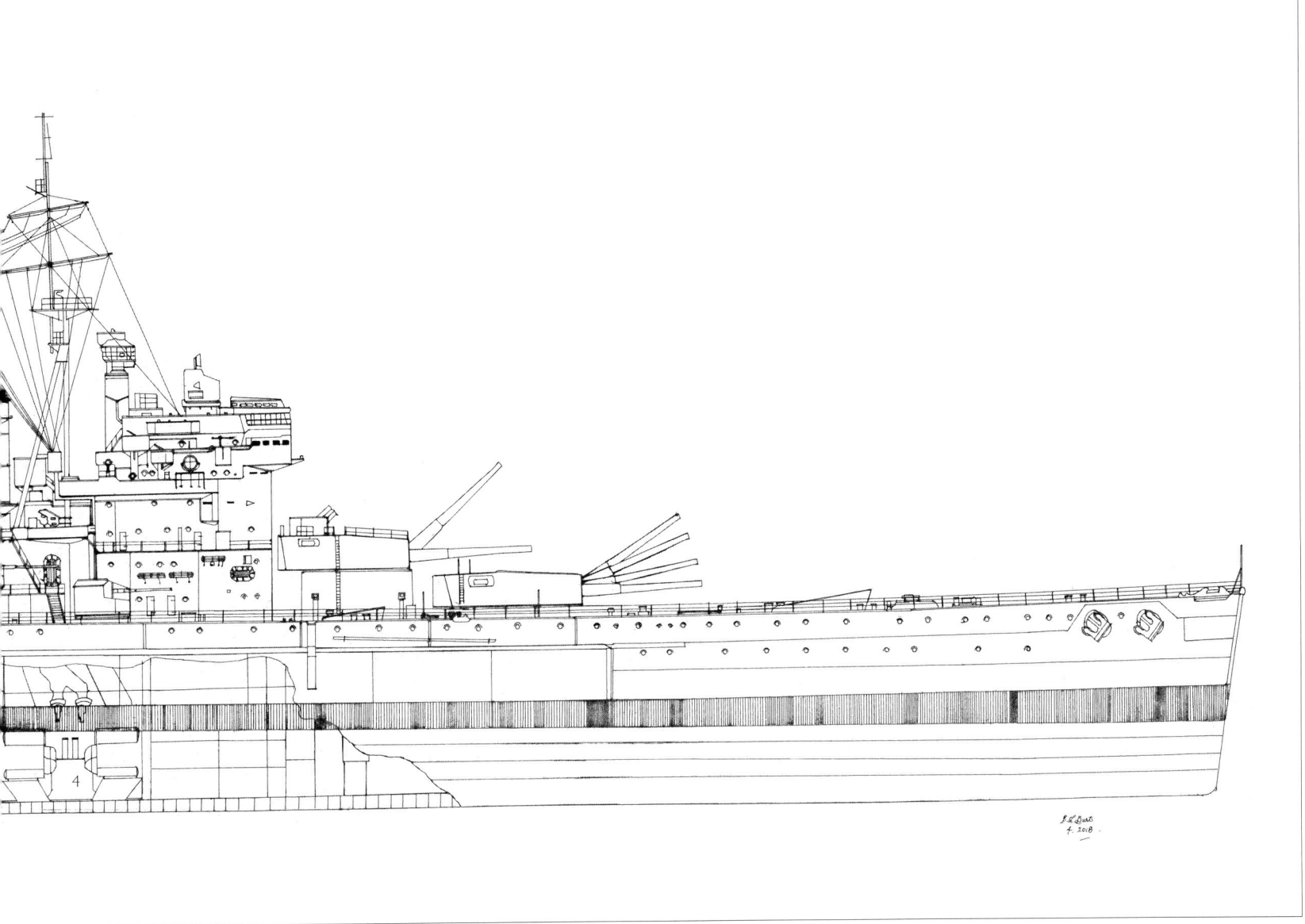

difficult to find a solution for a balanced design on a limited displacement.

At a Sea Lords meeting in October 1937 the following notes were recorded:

> It was decided that D.N.C. should prepare more accurate drawings of an 8 x 16in gun ship showing one or two alternatives for consideration, with aircraft provision if practicable, secondary armament of 12 x 5.25in guns, speed of 28 knots in the standard condition and protection as in *King George V*.
>
> Since that date it has been ascertained that two new turret designs, viz, a triple 16in and a twin 16in could not be prepared and the mountings delivered in time for ships ordered in the financial year 1938, and D.N.C. was instructed verbally by Controller to consider the design of 9 x 16in gun ship.

The limitations of the naval treaty in force at the time were 35,000 tons but a 9 x 16in-gunned new ship similar to a *King George V* would be around 36,150 tons. An alternative would be to drop the aircraft installation from the design which would bring the displacement down to about 35,500 tons which was seen to be more acceptable.

Further development over the next several months, with slight increases in ship size and gun calibre, saw a suitable layout which in fact was an improved *King George V* with 16in guns (see table).

A general description of the new ships for the 1938 programme was as follows:

The ships are designed to a standard displacement of 40,000 tons. The new displacement for capital ships is 45,000 tons but great Britain informed all the Naval Treaty powers that it is not intended that British capital ships shall, at present, exceed 40,000 tons. The mean draught varies from 30ft in the standard condition to about 33ft in the deep condition. In order to attain the required speed under width restrictions imposed by Portsmouth and Rosyth docks, a form having a square cut stern has been adopted.

The main armament consists of 9 x 16in guns in triple turrets, two, one superimposed above the other, are arranged forward and one aft. These guns fire a 2,357lb shell as compared with a 2,048lb shell carried in 'Nelson' and 'Rodney'; magazines and shell rooms are of sufficient size to enable 100 rounds per gun to be stowed. The secondary and long range anti-aircraft armament consists of 16 x 5.25in in 8 twin mountings arranged in four groups, forward and aft, port and starboard. The close range anti-aircraft armament consists of 6 x 2pdr Mk.M.8 barrel pom-poms all on the fixed structure. Magazine space is sufficient for 1,800 rounds per barrel.

14in Mk III quad gun turret for *King George V* class

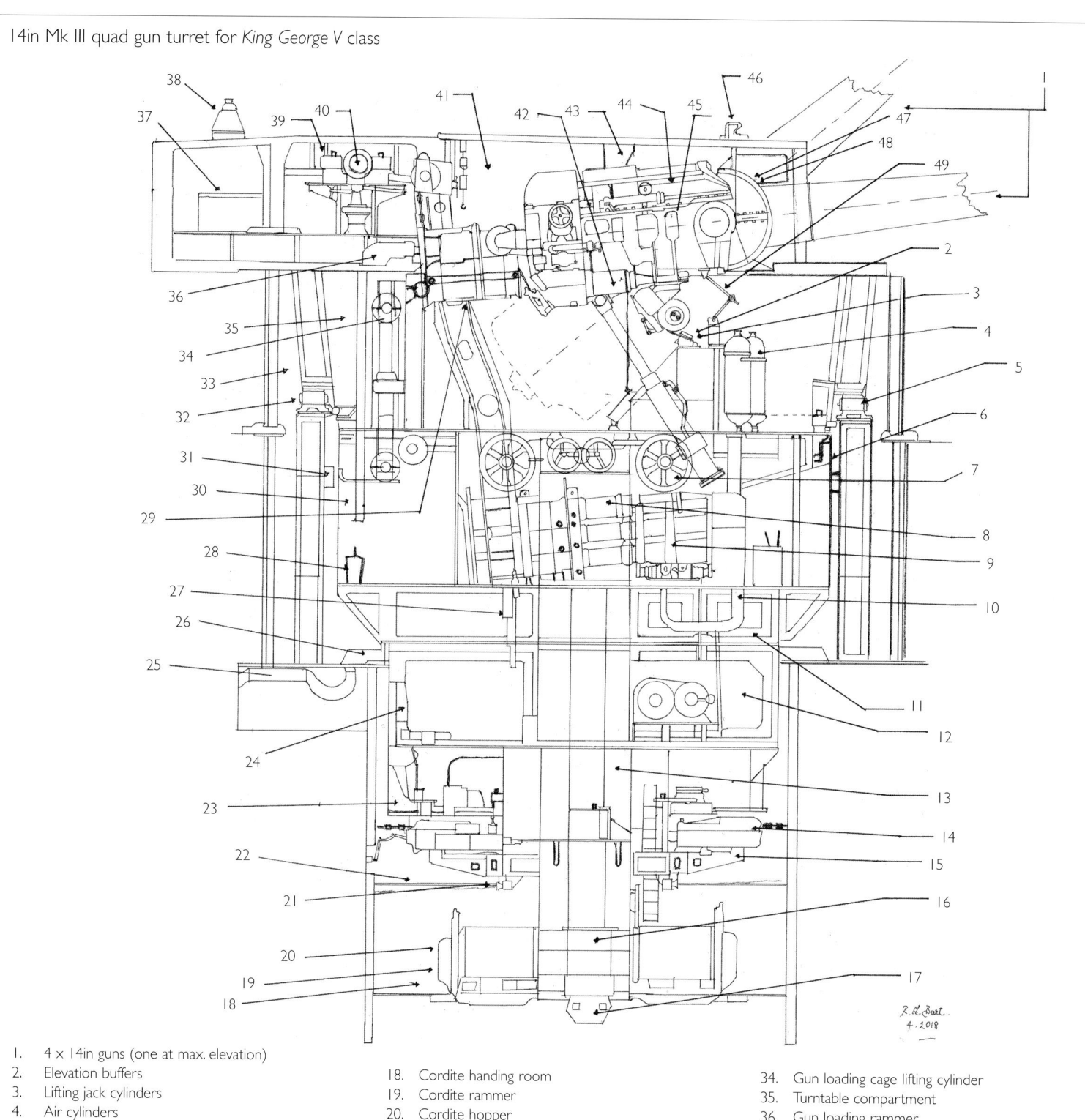

1. 4 × 14in guns (one at max. elevation)
2. Elevation buffers
3. Lifting jack cylinders
4. Air cylinders
5. Turntable rollers
6. Depression control cams
7. Central ammunition cage lifting winch
8. Bridge trays
9. Traverser
10. Rammer traverser to gun loading hoist
11. Training gear space
12. Training engine space
13. Central ammunition hoist
14. Revolving shell ring
15. Shell cage
16. Cordite cage
17. Centre pivot
18. Cordite handing room
19. Cordite rammer
20. Cordite hopper
21. Trunk spring guide rollers
22. Shell handing room
23. Revolving shell ring and shell rammer control
24. Shell rammer cylinders
25. Cable leads to turret
26. Cable platform gear
27. Rammer (ammunition) to traverser hoist
28. Striking down control standard
29. Gun loading cage
30. Working chamber
31. Training rack
32. Vertical guide roller
33. Turret buffer
34. Gun loading cage lifting cylinder
35. Turntable compartment
36. Gun loading rammer
37. Navigating cabinet ('A' Turret only)
38. Periscope
39. Roof supports
40. Rangefinder
41. Gunhouse
42. Recoil cylinder
43. Roof support
44. Run out cylinder
45. Cradle
46. Officer lookout periscope
47. Splinter screen
48. Gun protection chock
49. Walking pipes

INTRODUCTION

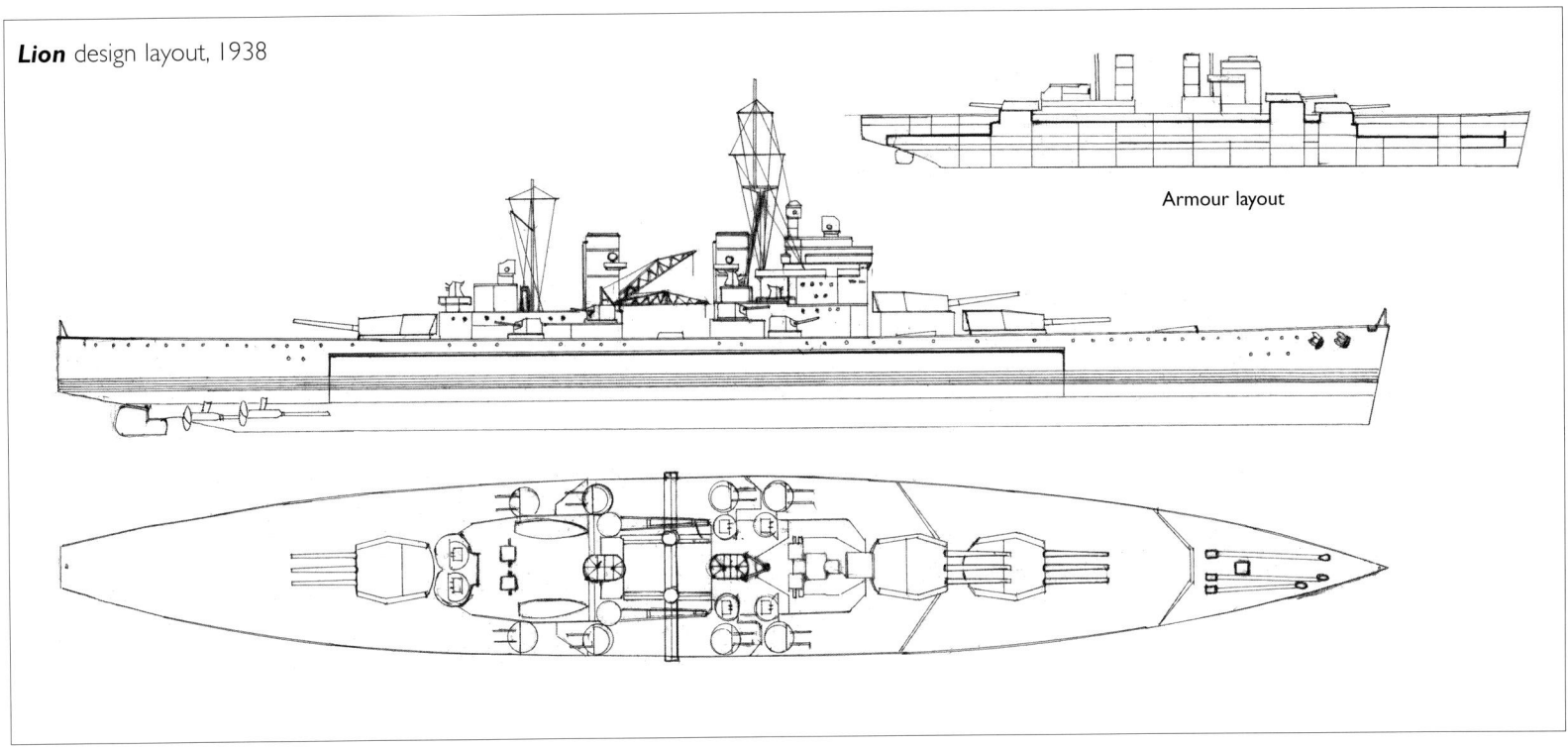

Lion design layout, 1938

Armour layout

LEGEND OF PARTICULARS FOR HMS *LION* AND *TEMERAIRE*, 1938

Standard displacement:	40,000 tons.
Length:	740ft (pp), 780ft (wl), 785ft (oa).
Beam:	105ft.
Draught:	30ft standard, 33ft 6in deep.
Freeboard:	28ft 3in forward, 22ft 3in amidships, 24ft 3in aft.
SHP:	120,000/130,000.
Number of shafts:	4.
Speed:	29¼ knots, 28¼ knots.
Total oil fuel capacity:	3,720 tons.
Endurance:	14,000 miles @ 10 knots.
Complement:	(as Fleet Flagship) 1,680.

Armament
9 x 16in (60rpg)
16 x 5.25in (150rpg)
6 x 8-barrel 2pdr (500 rounds per barrel).
Torpedoes: none.
Aircraft: 1 x D.111.H .catapult, 2 aircraft.

Armour
Ship's side over magazines and shell rooms:	15in above water with 15–5½in once below water.
Gun positions:	16in turrets 15–10–7in, roofs 6in.
Decks:	6–5in over machinery with 5–4in elsewhere.
Splinter protection:	1½–2in.
5.25in casemates:	½–1in.
Underwater protection:	1¾in and sandwich bulge.

Weights
Hull:	15,010 tons
Armour and protection:	14,180 tons
Armament:	7,100 tons
Machinery:	3,160 tons
General equipment:	1,100 tons
Standard displacement:	40,550 tons
	(includes 550 tons Board Margin)

The armament controls comprise 2 main director control tower, one forward on the bridge structure and one aft and 1 aft on Y turret; 4 T.S.I directors for H.A.L.A. armament, 2 forward and 2 aft; and 6 pom-pom directors.

Aircraft: A double acting fixed athwartship D.111.H. catapult between funnels. 2 aircraft carried in hangar built abreast the forward funnel. 2 cranes are provided for handling aircraft and boats.

Machinery consists of geared turbines driving 4 shafts in four engine rooms and 4 boiler rooms.

The machinery is designed to develop 120,000/130,000shp giving an estimated speed of 28 to 29 knots.

Oil fuel provided is 3,720 tons.

Protection: The arrangement of protection incorporates the results of the various experiments carried out in recent years. The underwater protection has been designed to withstand the explosion of a charge of 1,000lbs TNT. The side armour extends 8ft 6in below the standard waterline to main deck level – a total depth of about 23ft. The main deck is armoured throughout the citadel and is 6in thick.

The above design was fully developed and two vessels (*Lion* and *Temeraire*) were laid down in the summer of 1939 (see table).

A large amount of this design naturally went into the following *Vanguard*. In fact *Vanguard* was in all essentials a slightly improved *Lion* with four twin 15in turrets and the added benefit of war experience which was introduced into the vessel as it became available.

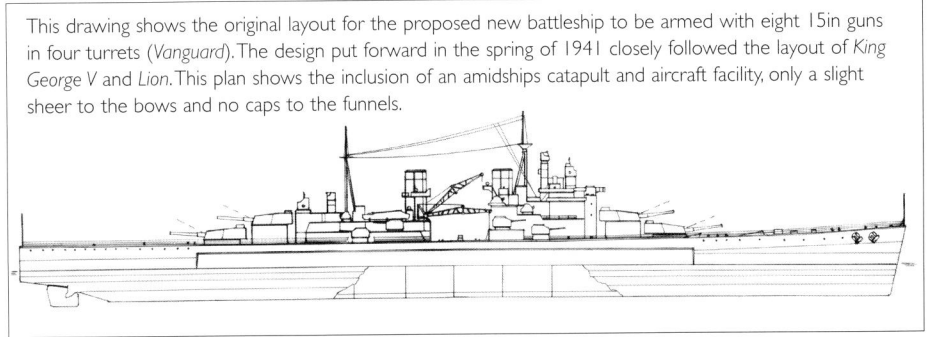

This drawing shows the original layout for the proposed new battleship to be armed with eight 15in guns in four turrets (*Vanguard*). The design put forward in the spring of 1941 closely followed the layout of *King George V* and *Lion*. This plan shows the inclusion of an amidships catapult and aircraft facility, only a slight sheer to the bows and no caps to the funnels.

Design and Construction

On 3 March 1939 a document was circulated amongst the Admiralty departments by the Director of Plans proposing the use of old naval heavy guns in storage in a single new-construction battleship. The proposal received a great deal of scrutiny but in general was accepted with some reservations and further investigation was requested. A letter from the DNC department reads as follows:

> It is difficult to remark on this proposition without some estimate of the time and money that would be saved and without an assurance that the taking up of these four 15in turret mountings will not prejudice the reserve of spare mountings for the Fleet. It is presumed that these mountings would be converted Mk 1N turrets, capable of taking the new heavy 15in projectiles.
>
> For a simultaneous war against Germany and Japan our inferiority in the Far East does not admit of improvement by further considerable naval expansion even if this were financially possible since other powers would automatically increase their Fleets and the vicious circle remain.
>
> Our Far Eastern problem would be greatly simplified by some assurance as to the attitude of the USA, who's Far Eastern interests would be as much menaced as ours in the event of Japanese attack.
>
> The advantages of possessing another fast heavy ship at an earlier date and presumably lower cost than would otherwise be possible are obvious.
>
> Against this may be set the following considerations:
>
> 1. The possibility of Japan keeping step with us.
> 2. The wisdom of putting old mountings in a new hull.
> 3. The desirability of building a ship that would be dissimilar to the rest of the Fleet with the possible exception of the *Hood*.
> 4. The possibility of delay in the provision of gun mountings for the secondary armament.
> 5. The manning problem.

The DNC, S V Goodall, replied on 10 March stating that a ship carrying four twin 15in turrets, protection and speed as in *King George V*, would have a displacement of 37,000 tons and cost about £7,000,000. This would not include the cost of the guns and mountings but only the cost of bringing them up to modern standards. The deciding factor in such a project would be the manufacture of the armour plates but in general it was accepted that the new ship could be completed in about 3½ years.

With all this in hand, further investigations were called for but when students of naval history take a look at Admiralty records regarding the concept of the *Vanguard* they will be forgiven for wondering how on earth the vessel was ever completed.

Against a background of severe agitation for further battleship construction during the Second World War, *Vanguard* was the only British battleship laid down and completed for service during this period. Her design was closely linked to that of the previous class of battleship (the *Lion* class of 1938) and incorporated as much of the experience and modern features that the Royal Navy construction departments could possibly fit into a vessel on a given limited displacement.

The Admiralty record of *Vanguard*'s design in the Ship's Cover is very brief:

> She was actually designed from the outcome of a proposal put forward by the D.N.C. Sir Stanley Goodall for the construction of a single battleship to be armed with 15in guns and mountings removed from HMS *Courageous* and *Glorious* when converted into aircraft carriers in 1924/30 and which could be rapidly completed before the *Lion* class which were at the time (8.2.1939) still in hand. The ship could be available to meet any emergency in the West or join the Eastern Fleet which it was proposed to organise if Japan should enter the war.

Three designs ('15A', '15B', '15C') were submitted on 17 July 1939 with displacements ranging from 38,000 tons to 40,000 tons. An extra design based on '15A' was proposed following a staff meeting on 27 February 1940 which included further modifications by fitting 2in to 2½in protection to the new ship's sides once abaft the citadel and called '15D'. More improvements in the way of protection were also made to the secondary 5.25in armament and the anti-aircraft gun battery was increased. The beam of the ship was increased from 105ft to 108ft (see table) to provide extra spaces for anti-torpedo measures within the hull.

In May 1939, during negotiations for the design, the DNC also asked for some consideration toward fitting an extra rudder, possibly 100–150ft from the bow, in case of damage to the main aft rudder from shell or torpedo. He also asked if it was at all possible that the ship might be steered by propellers alone. Following this suggestion, some tests were carried out by the Admiralty Experiment Works at Haslar, but these tests seem to have revealed little as to the suitability of such additions to any new design and the subject was dropped.

The conclusion of a rather lengthy debate was that the '15D' design proved acceptable to Their Lordships and all concerned with the design were given instructions to proceed and develop it. Although the design was approved on 20 May 1940 work was temporarily suspended in June of that year but resumed again in October. Further modifications to remove any aircraft equipment were sanctioned. On 17 April 1941 the final approval for the design – now called '15E' – was given.

The ship was laid down in October 1941 but the next few months were to show that more urgent requirements such as anti-submarine vessels and the ever-changing demands of war from the air made it impossible to realise the original intention for early completion and *Vanguard*'s construction had reduced to a very slow pace indeed. In fact, battleship construction had come under severe criticism both from the Admiralty and the Government.

In early 1942 it was pointed out by the Controller that it was practically impossible to give a firm date for the ship's completion. Moreover, in June of that year the Construction Committee were looking at the possibility of turning the new battleship into a much-needed aircraft carrier, a type of ship which was proving itself to be the most important in the current war. A letter was sent to all concerned in September 1942:

> Preliminary consideration has been given to the possibility of converting *Vanguard* to an aircraft carrier. The conversion presents no fundamental difficulties and the general lines of the 1942 Fleet carrier could be followed. The design could be completed six months after approval to convert and the ship could complete by early 1946 assuming approval is given in October 1942.
>
> The machinery would be substantially unaltered and could proceed.
>
> The oil stowage of *Vanguard* is at present 4,850 tons and it

DESIGN AND CONSTRUCTION

would probably be not possible to increase this beyond 570 tons without waste of material and delay.

Structural material could be used to a large extent and the armour for *Vanguard* as a battleship has been accelerated to take advantage of a gap in production and is fairly well advanced. Considerable waste is to be expected if the ship is finished as an aircraft carrier. It would probably be advantageous to fit the armoured deck forward and aft as for a battleship.

Staff requirements regarding thickness of lower hangar deck and flight deck armour will affect the work to be done on the present main deck armour.

The manufacture of *Vanguard*'s armour is proceeding apace and wastage will be much aggravated unless a decision is quickly reached.

The possibility of this conversion has again been kept secret in this department as otherwise drawing work would suffer.

The firm (John Brown) have planned their labour work so that the large numbers of men employed in getting *Indefatigable* to the launching stage in December 1942 are to be fleeted over to *Vanguard* and progress her rapidly. This again emphasises the importance of an immediate decision.

This consideration of possible conversion was not the only obstacle for *Vanguard*. There was also the question of the large amount of skilled labour that was required for the construction of a battleship (John Brown had stated that it could move men from one ship to another quickly). It was a fact that the yard was suffering from severe shortages of skilled labour. Fortunately within a short period of time, and against vociferous opposition from both the First Sea Lord Sir Dudley Pound and the Prime Minister Winston Churchill to conversion to an aircraft carrier, the suggestion was dropped. (Also by this time the Royal Navy had lost five capital ships.) After this hiatus the construction of *Vanguard* continued but at a very slow pace.

During her construction *Vanguard* was to benefit from wartime experience and the loss of the battleship *Prince of Wales* on 10 December 1941 had the biggest impact. After a lengthy enquiry the following improvements were introduced into *Vanguard* from September 1942:

1. Closely subdivided watertight compartments arranged on the lower deck over the sandwich protection in lieu of wash places and stores.
2. 5.25in transfer positions in the supply to No 2 and 3 mountings, port and starboard were arranged on the middle deck instead of on the lower deck.
3. Trunked access to compartments occupied in action to be arranged within the citadel as far as far as space permits.
4. Substantial reduction in the number of scuttles below the weather deck.

Further improvements carried out at the same time were:

1. An increase in the number of diesel generators from two to four and a reduction in turbo generators from six to four.
2. Increase in sheer to the bows and anchor stowage recessed into the hull.
3. Addition of one SG radar set on the after DCT, WSR radar set on the foretop and main-armament barrage directors.
4. Omission of bulk stowage of petrol; all boats to be diesel driven.
5. Increase of oil fuel stowage.
6. Design of machinery for economy at high power including omission of cruising turbines.
7. Re-arrangement of W/T office to give bridge receiving room, transmitter room in aft superstructure and a protected transmitter room.

NEW DESIGNS (*VANGUARD*) COMPARED WITH *KING GEORGE V* AND *LION* CLASSES

	'15A' (1939)	'15B' (1939)	'15C' (1939)	Lion	King George V
Displacement:	38,000 tons	40,000 tons	40,000 tons	40,000 tons	35,000 tons
Length (oa):	775ft	805ft	805ft	785ft	745ft
Beam:	104ft	105ft	105ft	105ft	104ft
Draught:	29ft	29ft 9in	29ft 9in	30ft	26ft
SHP:	110,000	143,000	130,000	130,000	110,000
Speed:	29 knots	29¼ knots	28¼ knots	28¼ knots	28 knots
Oil:	3,700 tons	3,700 tons	3,700 tons	3,700 tons	3,700 tons
Endurance:	14,000 @ 10 knots	As in '15A'	As in '15A'	As in '15A'	14,000 @ 10 knots
Complement:	1,600 (Improved *KGV*)	As in '15A' (Improved *KGV*)	As in '15A' (*Lion* development)	As in '15A'	1,645

'15D' COMPARED WITH *LION* CLASS, 1940

	'15D'	Lion
Displacement:	41,200 tons	40,000 tons
Length (pp/wl/oa):	760/800/809ft	740/780/785ft
Beam:	105ft 6in	105ft
Draught:	30–33ft	30–33ft
SHP:	130,000	130,000
Speed:	29–30¼ knots	29–30¼ knots
Oil:	3,900 tons	3,720 tons
Armament:	8 × 15in	9 × 16in
	16 × 5.25in	16 × 5.25in

8. Addition of Oerlikon mounting positions to be fixed when the upper deck arrangements are more definite.
9. To be fitted as Fleet Flagship.
10. Addition of L.A. Directors for night control of secondary armament.
11. Trunked access to compartments outside citadel.
12. Addition of Asdics.
13. Increased longitudinal separation of inner and outer propellers.
14. Addition of splinter protection on sides of magazines.
15. Sick bay to be arranged partly below armour.
16. Additional breakwater immediately before 'A' 15in turret.
17. An increase in pom-pom gun ammunition necessitated the crown of the highest magazine in block 222 to 247 being at the lower deck level, to be given 1¼in NC splinter protection.

By December 1942, however, amid severe wartime conditions, her construction had virtually stopped with most shipbuilding resources being directed to smaller craft. Also the two new battleships *Lion* and *Temeraire* already on the stocks were due to be cancelled. On hearing of this situation Churchill sent a letter to the Admiralty:

> You have put the completion date for this ship back at least 18 months. If she is not to be fit for service till March 31 1946 the whole question of her future construction must be reviewed.
>
> I am greatly concerned at the way she has been cast aside. Pray let me have a statement showing various estimates you have for the dates of completion of this ship since I left the Admiralty.

On 12 January 1943 the First Lord of the Admiralty A V Alexander replied:

> With regard to the *Vanguard*, the Controller is looking into the matter again, but has already pointed out that it would not be possible at the present stage to give a firm date for completion.

VANGUARD: DESIGN AS IN 1941 AND ALTERED IN 1942

	1941	1942
Displacement:	41,600 tons	42,300 tons
Length (pp):	760ft	760ft
Length (wl):	800ft	800ft
Length (oa):	809ft	813ft
Freeboard forward:	32ft 6in	36ft 8in
Freeboard amidships:	23ft	22ft 8in
Freeboard aft:	25ft	24ft 8in
Draught:	33ft	33ft 10in
Complement:	1,600	1,710
Armament:	8 × 15in	8 × 15in
	16 × 5.25in	16 × 5.25in
	6 × 2pdr Mk VII pom-poms	9 × 2pdr
	1 × 2pdr Mk VII	
	12 × Oerlikons	
Aircraft:	1	0
Weights (tons)		
Hull	16,100	16,500
Armour	15,200	15,350
Armament	5,950	6,100
Machinery	3,250	3,150
General equipment	1,100	1,200

VANGUARD ORIGINAL LEGEND, SEPTEMBER 1942

Deep displacement:	50,074 tons
Hull:	17,000 tons
Armour:	15,265 tons
Armament:	7,310 tons
Machinery:	3,160 tons
Fuel:	4,930 tons
Equipment:	1,819 tons
Feedwater:	350 tons
Lubricating oil:	30 tons
Water protection (abreast 'Y' turret):	110 tons
Draught at FP:	33ft 6¾in
Draught at AP:	35ft ½in
GM:	9.12ft
Range of stability:	72 degrees
Maximum GZ:	5.4ft
Light condition:	43,711 tons
Provisions:	403 tons
Anchor cables:	179 tons
Cranes:	90 tons
Masts, rigging etc:	77 tons
General mess stores:	42 tons
Officers' mess:	30 tons
Canteen stores:	20 tons

Armament

Revolving weight of 'A', 'B', 'X' 'Y' 15in turrets:	3,420 tons
5.25in mountings, spares and pumps etc:	559 tons
6 Mk V IA pom-poms, ammunition and directors, 10 Bofors and 1 STAAG mounting:	559 tons
Hydraulic machinery:	130 tons
15in directors (2):	70 tons

Armour

Protectional bulkhead:	1,454 tons
Splinter protection to magazines:	721 tons
Conning tower:	78 tons
5.25in casemates:	384 tons
Plating to bridge:	207 tons
After emergency CT:	69 tons
DCT:	38 tons

I have discovered that the Future Building Committee in the Admiralty is even discussing at the present time whether it would not be better strategically to turn the *Vanguard* hull into an armoured aircraft carrier which would give us an armoured aircraft carrier earlier than either of the *Ark Royal*s.

This proposal gave me a bit of a shock in view of the strong desire you have expressed to get this powerful battleship into commission as soon as possible. It has been pointed out to me that if the *Vanguard* goes ahead and lasts 20 years, the gun turrets will then be nearly 50 years old. The question of finding a large quantity of additional skilled labour sufficient to speed up the completion of the ship is one of great difficulty. At the moment therefore the matter is being further enquired into. We are continuing to give priority to Escort ships. I will send you another report as soon as possible.

Moreover, the builders John Brown had pointed out that the *Vanguard* was not being worked on by a full complement of workers but at that stage she was being attended by a sufficient number of platers which would be stepped up when the carrier *Indefatigable* was launched. It was put forward that only the highest-skilled men could be allowed to work on the battleship and as stated before such men were in very short supply indeed.

More correspondence and debate followed from various departments but at the end of it the conclusion was that *Vanguard*'s construction should be continued as best as possible with the limited resources until the process could be accelerated.

From the laying down of her keel plates through to her launch, *Vanguard* was been on the stocks for three years. The following table shows her construction procedure:

March 1939:	First proposal for ship armed with spare 15in guns etc.
July 1939:	Design investigated and submitted.
March 1940:	Further investigations into design.
May 1940:	Early design approved.
March 1941:	An order for a battleship design placed with the shipyard of John Brown.
24 March 1941:	Drawings and early requirements forwarded to John Brown.
April 1941:	Approval for Design '15E'.
2 October 1941:	Keel plates laid down.
3 November 1941:	John Brown was informed that the ship was to be called *Vanguard* but on no account was to be revealed to the general public.
1942 to 1944:	Slow construction with some small alterations to the design.
30 November 1944:	*Vanguard* launched.
December 1944 to 1946:	Construction at accelerated pace.
25 April 1946:	Commissioned for early sea trials.
8 August 1946:	Final acceptance trials completed.

DESIGN AND CONSTRUCTION

Left: At the 'hush-hush' launch of Britain's newest battleship, Princess Elizabeth pressed the electric button and cut the ribbon with a pair of silver scissors to start the process. A bottle of Empire red wine broke across the bow and her personal standard broke out from the flagstaff, the first time this flag was used. It had been made for the Princess by the Royal Navy. Afterwards she said 'This will always serve to remind me that the first important public duty I ever undertook was a naval occasion.'

Launch, 30 November 1944

The fact that she had been on the stocks for such a long time and that there had been no British battleship launched since 1940 (the *King George V* class), *Vanguard*'s launch day was looked upon as rather special. Moreover, the ceremony was to be carried out by Her Royal Highness the Princess Elizabeth.

The Royal Family had requested that the ceremony was to be treated as a private function and no members of the general public be admitted unless they were officially invited. Being launched under wartime conditions, there was also the question of security affecting any information given to the press and public. The following statement was issued to the John Brown shipyard

> The question as to the date when details of the launch would be released to the general public would appear to be one for Board decision, observing that the general rule is that details are not normally given until at least one month after the commissioning of the vessel. In deciding on an early date for release it has to be borne in mind that should the existence of the vessel be published before the end of the European war and before the ship leaves the Clyde, the possibility of the enemy making a special bombing attack, though unlikely, cannot be ruled out.

Although this statement was issued in October 1944, a letter was sent to the press office on 29 November saying that the launch could be mentioned but with strict limits on actual information.

1. Nothing could be mentioned regarding the ship's name.
2. Nothing was to be said of the type or class of vessel beyond her being a battleship launched from a Northern shipyard.
3. There were no restrictions of taking photographs but photographers should note that any photo for immediate release should not include any person that would indicate the location of the shipyard.
4. After the launch the Royal guests will pose for photographs but shipyard personnel will step aside and not be included in the view.
5. Photographs showing fuller details will be filed for possible publication at a later date.

There were some anxious moments as the great ship took to the water for a strong wind blew up the river and in towards the basin. The waiting tugs, however, carried out their task with their usual skill and soon brought the great hull into position in the Clyde.

The Times takes up the story on 2 December 1944:

> Princess Elizabeth came here recently to name and launch our newest battleship, the greatest battleship yet built here in the British Isles, but the ship's name, type and class are for the present secret. The event was something of a landmark in the Princess's life. She is now 18 and as a preparation for her great destiny, she has for some little time been giving an increasingly important place to public or social occasions but never before has she travelled from London without the King and Queen to carry through the leading part in a ceremony of national importance. For the first time Princess Elizabeth's own Standard was flown (it was made for her by the Royal Navy). The flag was broken at the Flagship by two dockyard workers and she took her place on the launching platform and God Save the King was played. There was a short wait until the

Right: This photograph was issued for the press and as can be seen it is not giving much away. A rather dull photo and all salient features are hidden, but at the time of much secrecy it was thought to be necessary. Although not publicly named at the time of launch, the German Press Agency issued a statement a few weeks later stating that the British had just launched a new battleship to be named *Vanguard* and would be armed with nine 16in guns and displace over 45,000 tons.

Vanguard fitting out at the John Brown shipyard. During this period there was much speculation over her features and none more dramatic than the statement in the *Birmingham Daily Gazette* of December 1944: 'She is to be equipped with "electric eyes" to pierce the thickest fog and darkness in a way that no human eye could ever do, to see and detect the enemy position, speed and course.'

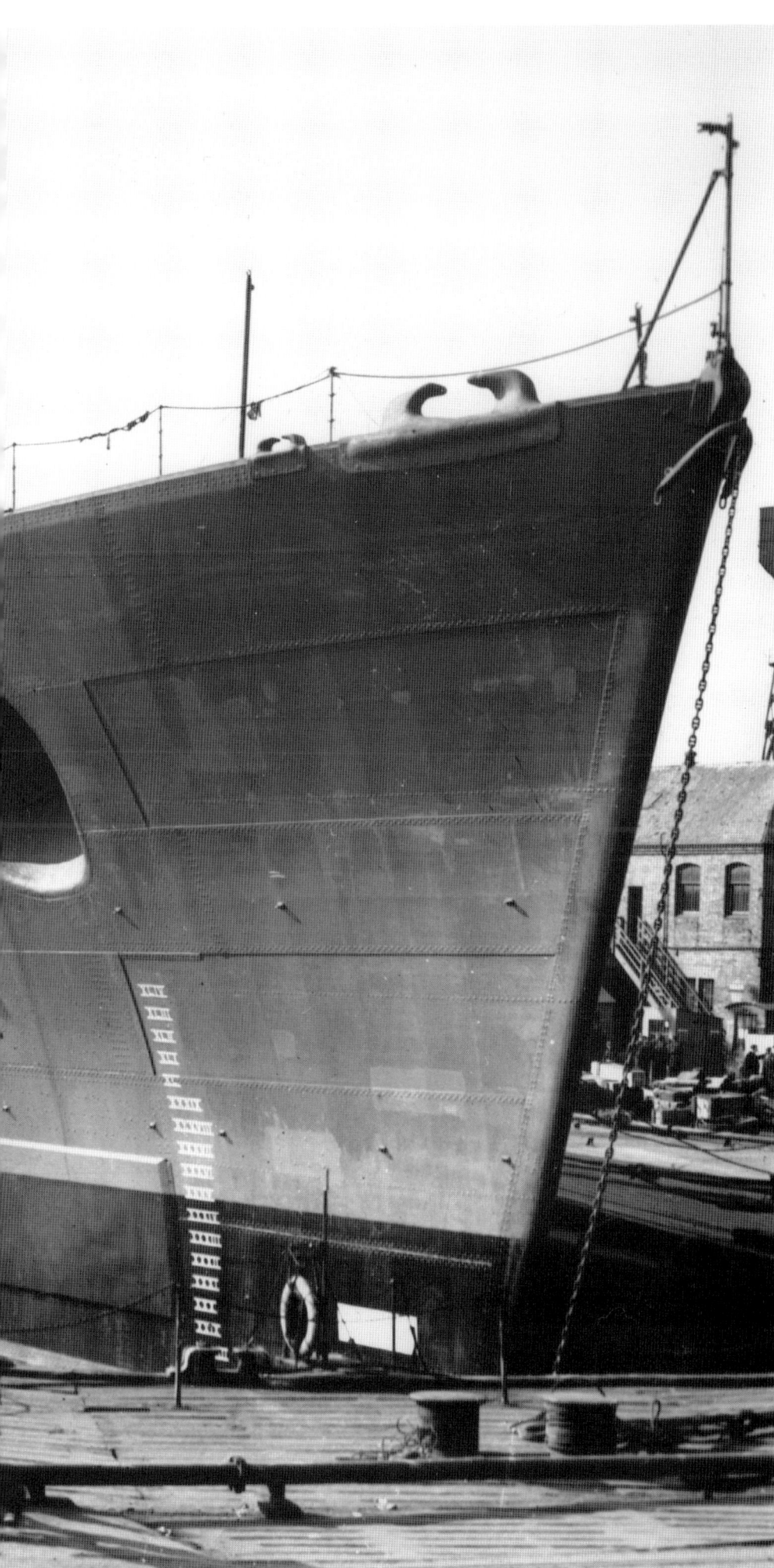

ship had been made ready to slide away and then Princess Elizabeth pressed the button which released the ship and at the same time let go the cord of a big ribboned bottle of Empire red wine which smashed against the hull. In a clear voice the Princess named her with a name which cannot yet be published and said 'May God Bless all who sail in her'. The ship moved smoothly and slowly away with figures waving and cheering on her decks. As her stern hit the water her Ensign was run up.

There are no official figures for her launch except for the following:

Displacement: 25,350 tons.
Draught: 15ft 6½in on the forward perpendicular
23ft 3¼in on the aft perpendicular.
Condition: No water on board.
Boilers fitted.
Only partial armour fitted.

Although no launch sheet is available for *Vanguard* there was some suggestion that she had more hog than sag than *King George V* which of course was understandable owing to her greater length and width of hull.

Right: *Vanguard* almost complete and preparing to leave the builder's yard for the first time. Seen from a starboard quarter angle which shows her complex aft superstructure very well. Note the aft DCT with Type 274 radar on top.

Vanguard
Inboard profile and sections, 1946

Frame 316 looking aft
1. Upper deck
2. Main deck
3. Middle deck
4. Lower deck
5. Platform deck
6. Prop shafts
7. Cabins
8. Lobby
9. Cabins
10. Capstan compartment
11. Stores
12. Pump room

Frame 289 looking aft
1. Upper deck
2. Main deck
3. Middle deck
4. Lower deck
5. Upper platform deck
6. Cabins
7. Officers' bathrooms
8. Lobby
9. Naval stores
10. Church
11. Midshipmen's compartment
12. Admiral's store
13. Ventilated flour store
14. Pump rooms
15. Marines' store
16. Feed water tanks
17. Shaft passages

Frame 211 looking aft
1. Admiral's bridge
2. No 1 platform
3. Boat deck
4. Shelter deck
5. Upper deck
6. Main deck
7. Middle deck
8. Lower deck
9. Platform deck
10. Hold
11. 5.25in hoist compartments
12. Upper transmitter room
13. Officers office
14. Office
15. Staff office
16. Chief of staff's day cabin
17. Wardroom

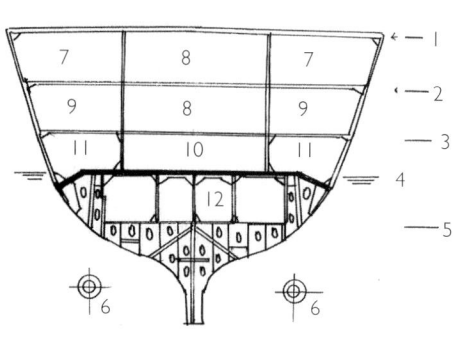
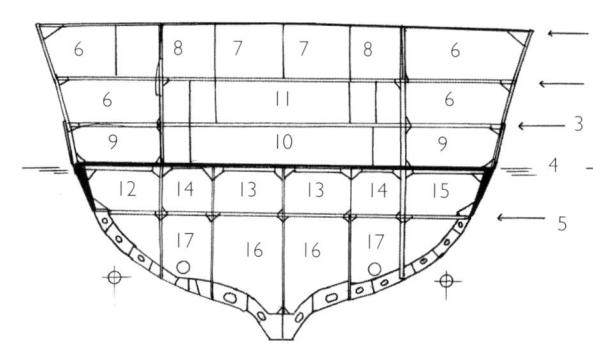
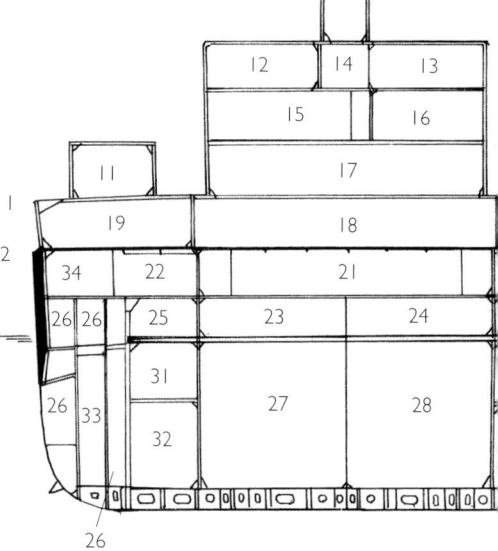
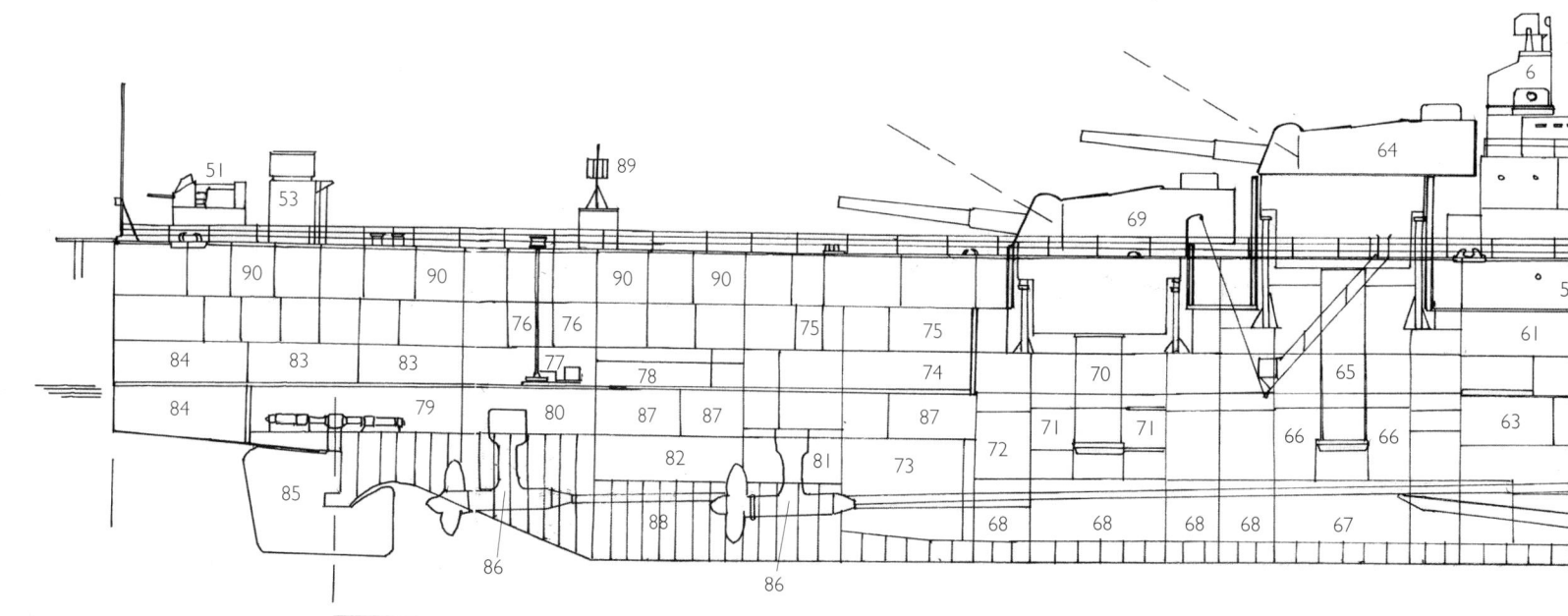

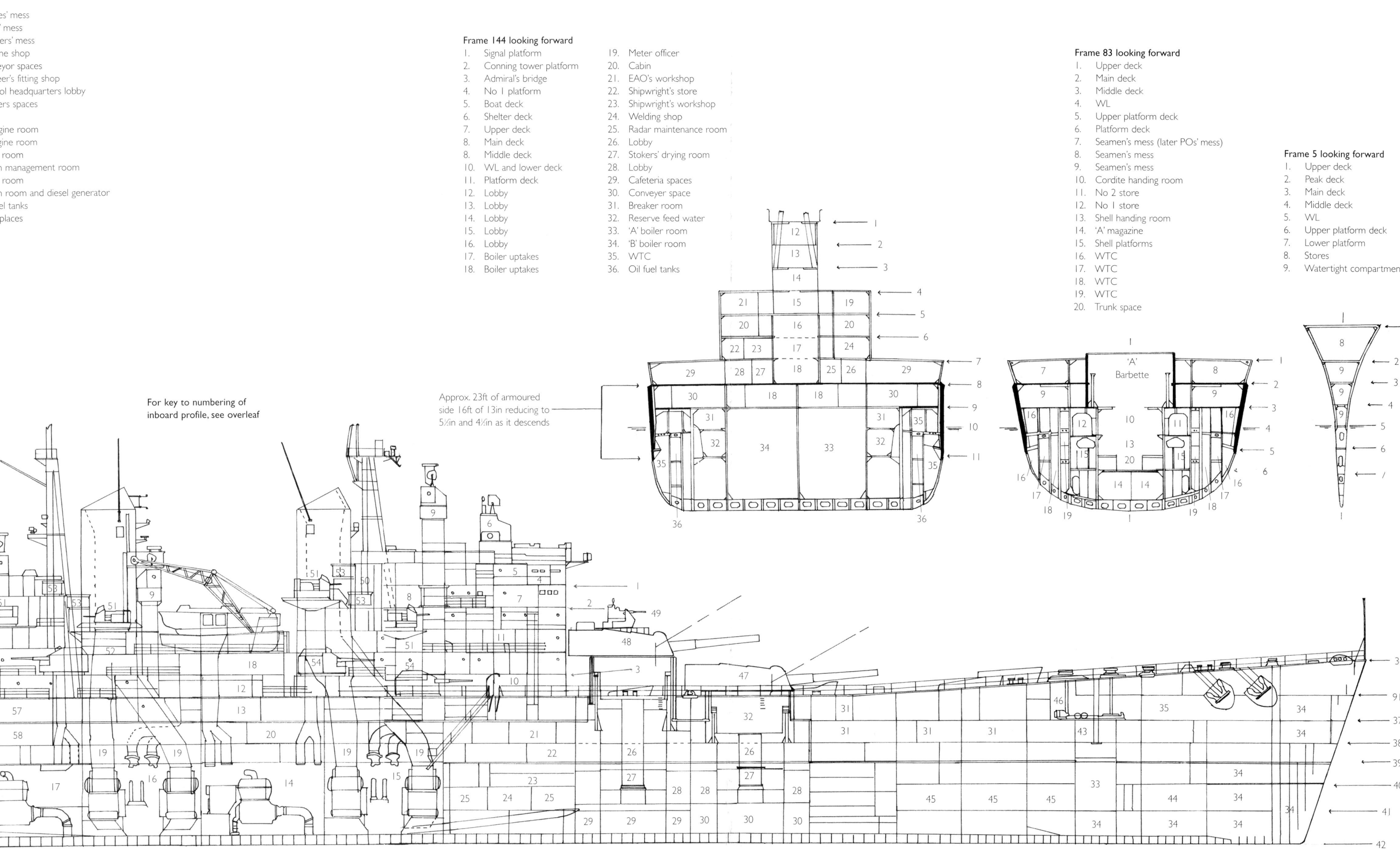

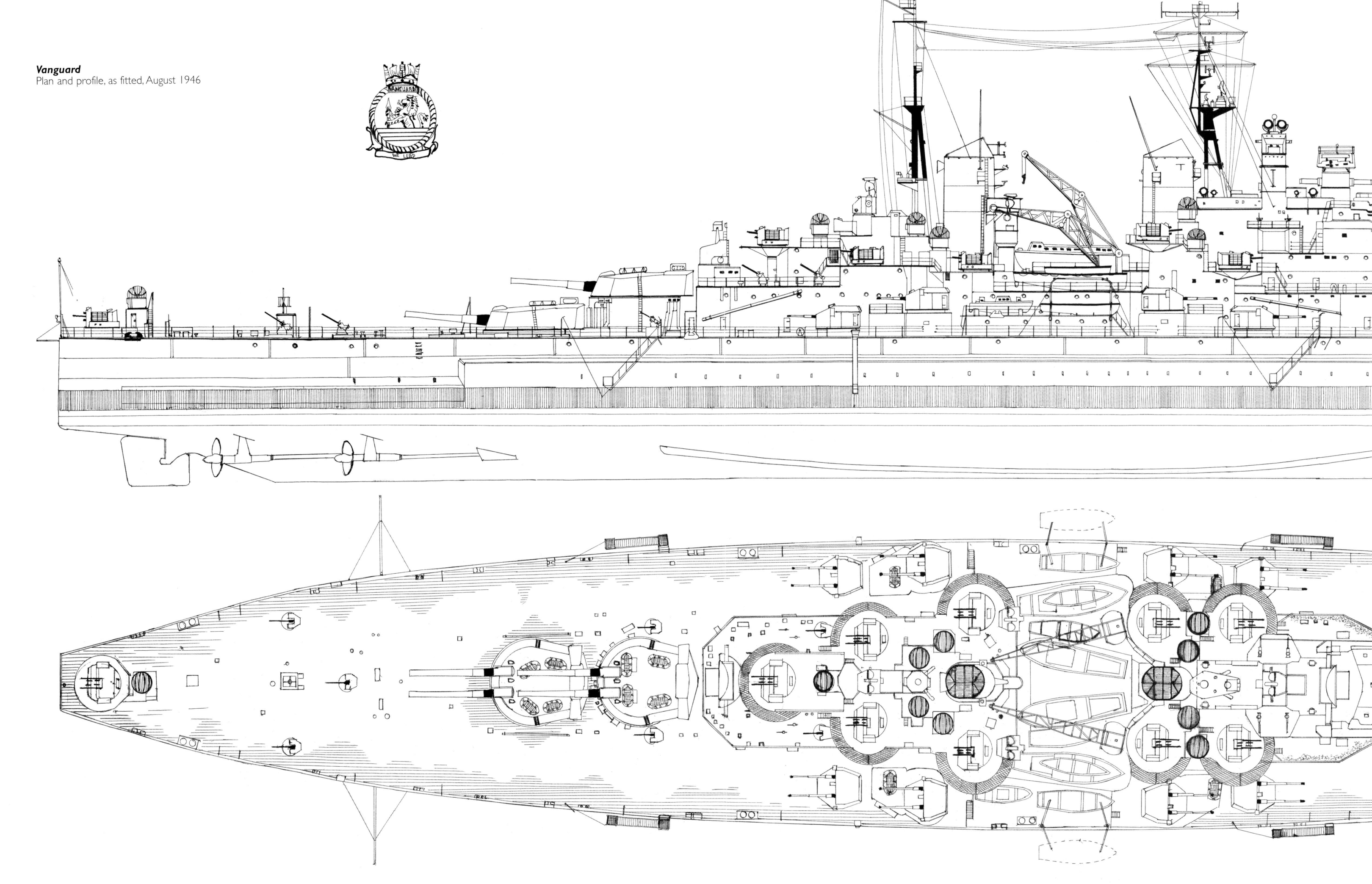

Vanguard
Plan and profile, as fitted, August 1946

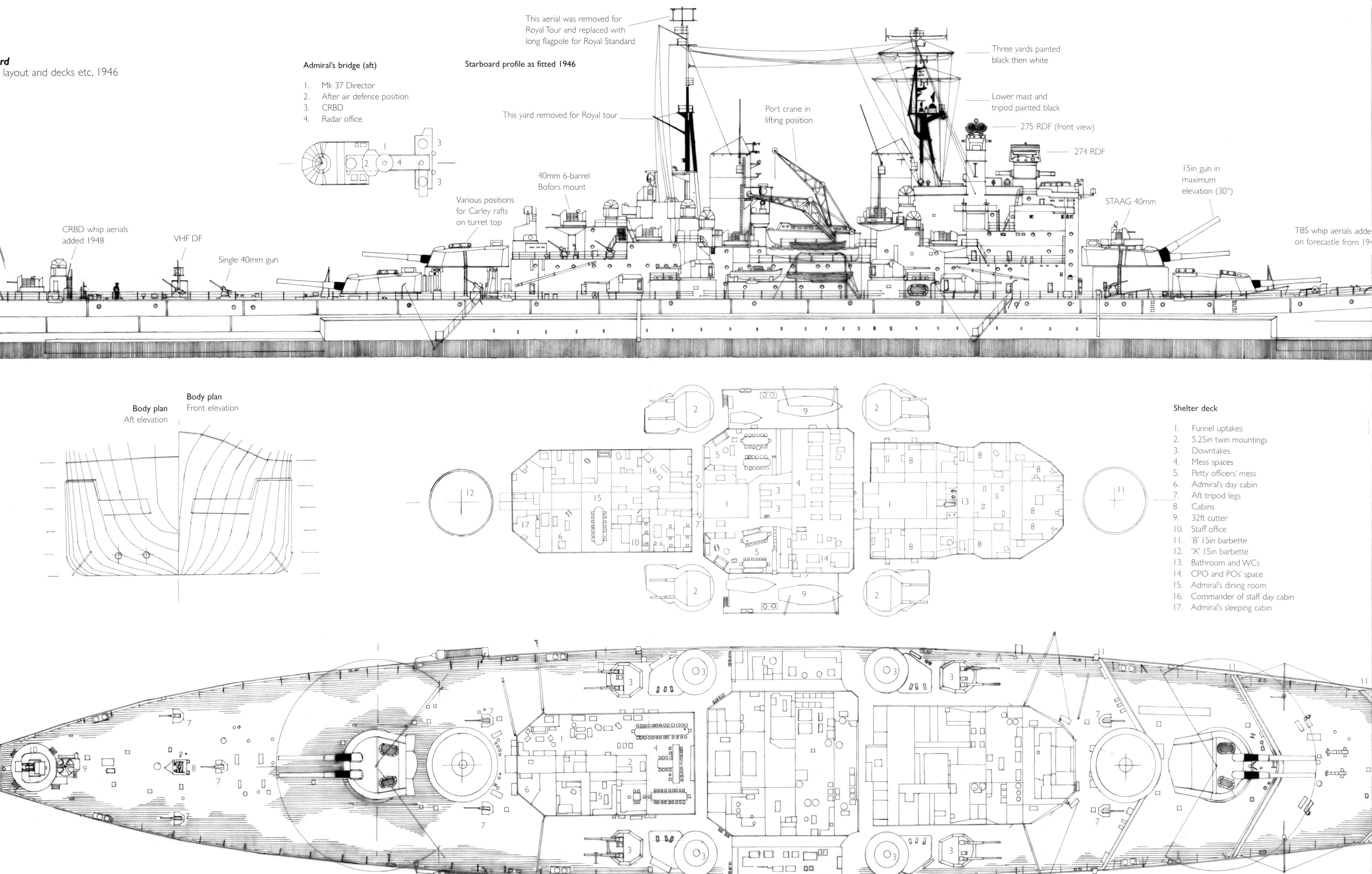

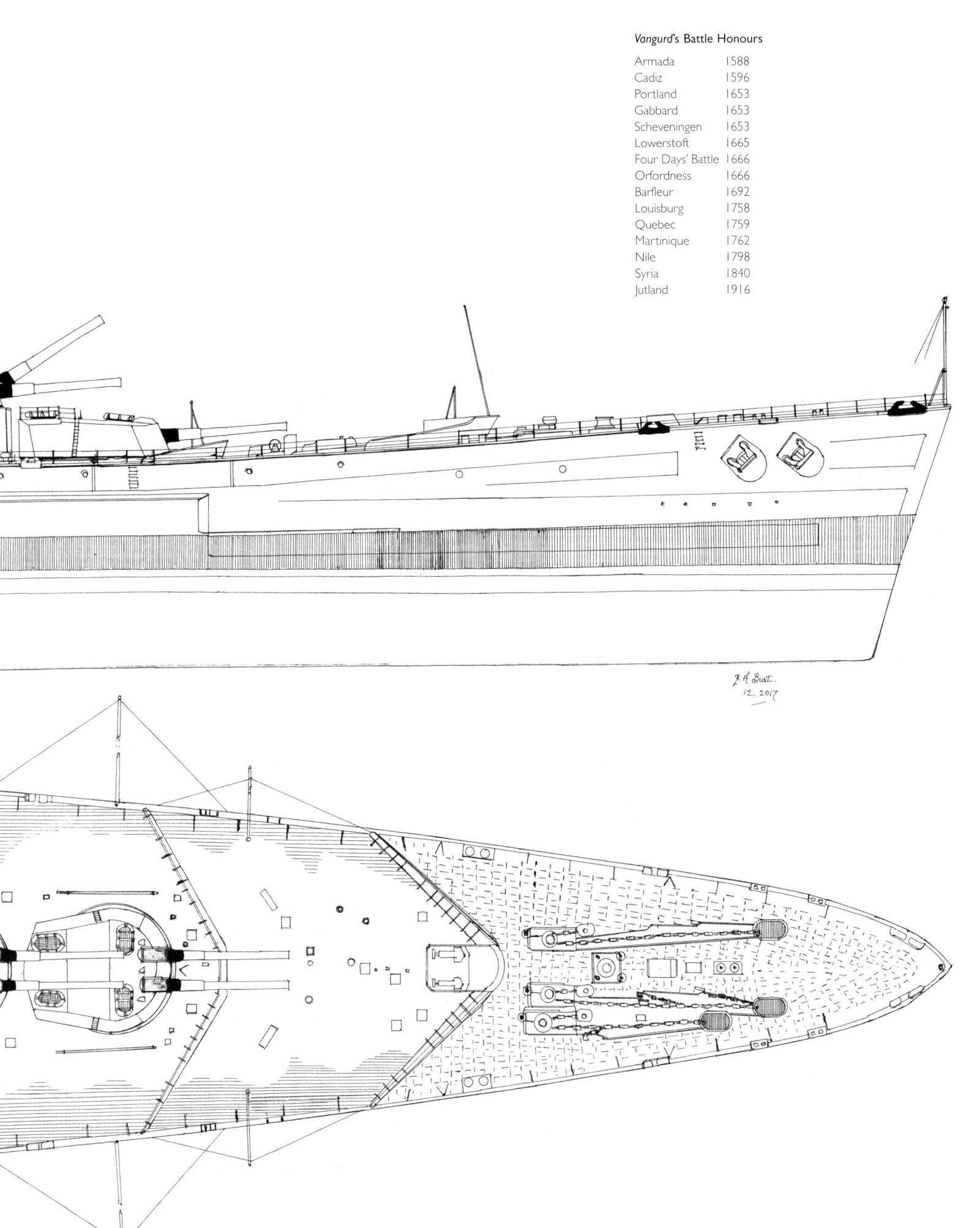

Vangurd's Battle Honours

Armada	1588
Cadiz	1596
Portland	1653
Gabbard	1653
Scheveningen	1653
Lowerstoft	1665
Four Days' Battle	1666
Orfordness	1666
Barfleur	1692
Louisburg	1758
Quebec	1759
Martinique	1762
Nile	1798
Syria	1840
Jutland	1916

Key to starboard inboard profile (overleaf)

1. Conning tower platform
2. Admiral's bridge
3. Shelter deck
4. Conning position
5. Captain's position and quarters
6. 15in gunnery control towers
7. Plotting office
8. Y office
9. Mk 37 Director
10. Galley
11. Cabins
12. Coppersmith's workshop
13. Cafeteria spaces
14. 'A'+'B' engine rooms
15. 'A'+'B' boiler rooms
16. 'Y'+'X' boiler rooms
17. 'Y'+'X' engine rooms
18. CPOs' cafeteria
19. Funnel uptakes
20. Damage control comp't
21. Sickbay
22. Radar display position
23. Transmitting station
24. Bofors magazine
25. 5.25in shell rooms
26. Cordite handing rooms (15in)
27. Shell handing rooms (15in)
28. 15in shell rooms
29. 'B' magazines
30. 'A' magazines
31. Seamen's messes
32. 'A' barbette
33. Cable locker
34. Watertight compartments
35. Crew's WCs
36. Upper deck
37. Main deck
38. Middle deck
39. Lower deck
40. Upper platform deck
41. Platform deck
42. Keel
43. Ship's study
44. Arctic clothing store
45. WTCs and spare gear etc.
46. Deck store
47. 'A' 15in twin turret
48. 'B' 15in twin turret
49. STAAG mounting
50. Signal house
51. Bofors mountings
52. Radar office
53. Close range barrage fire control (CR
54. 5.25in turrets
55. 5.25in shell rooms
56. 5.25in magazines
57. Mess spaces
58. Stokers' workplace and seamen's wa
59. Marines' cinema
60. Admiral's day cabin
61. Auxiliary medical distribution room
62. Washplaces
63. Bofors magazine
64. 'X' 15in twin turret
65. Cordite handing room
66. Shell handing room
67. 'X' magazine
68. 'Y' magazine
69. 'Y' 15in twin turret
70. Cordite handing room
71. Shell handing room
72. Shell rooms
73. Gland compartment and FW tanks
74. Church
75. Marine messes
76. Midshipmen's chest compartment
77. Capstan store
78. Clothing store and cool room
79. Steering gear compartment
80. Awning room
81. Spirit room
82. Warrant officers' stores and WTC
83. Stores
84. Watertight compartments
85. Rudder
86. Propeller shafts and brackets
87. WTC and marines' stores
88. Watertight compartments
89. High frequency directional finder
90. Cabins
91. Peak deck

Signal gunnery control and compass platform

1. DC tower position (15in)
2. Searchlight platform
3. Compass platform
4. Flag lockers and signal space
5. Wireless office

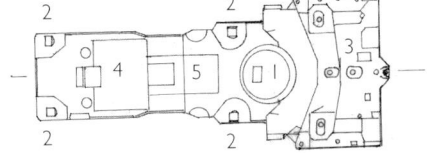

Conning tower platform

1. Downtakes
2. Captain's sea cabin
3. Captain's toilet and lobby
4. Charthouse
5. Conning tower
6. Signal house
7. Cabins

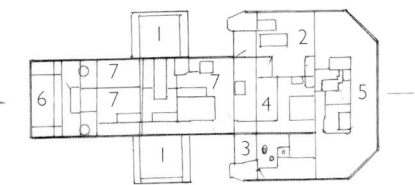

Admiral's bridge

1. 40mm Bofors
2. Funnel uptakes
3. Downtakes
4. Bridge
5. Staff rooms
6. Sliding windows in front of bridge
7. Metadyne room
8. Admiral's compass platform

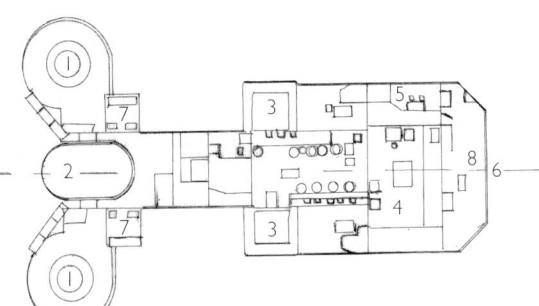

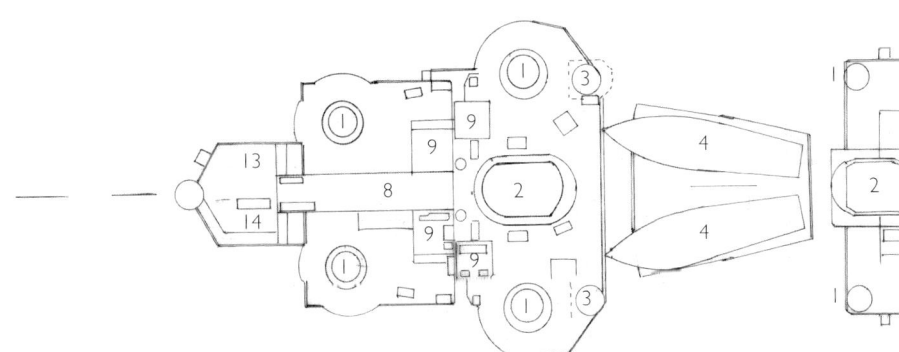
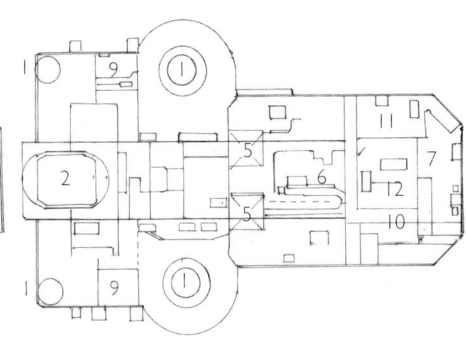

Upper deck

1. Wardroom anteroom
2. Lobby
3. 5.25in mounts
4. Wardroom
5. Pantry
6. Flag Lt's cabin
7. Single 40mm mounts
8. VHF DF
9. CRBD
10. 6-barrel 40mm mount
11. Breakwater
12. Metal chequer plating

No 1 Platform deck

1. 40mm Bofors
2. Funnel uptakes
3. Mk 37 Directors
4. Diesel picket boat
5. Downtakes
6. Various office spaces and cypher office
7. Admiral's sea cabin
8. Bofors magazine
9. Metadyne rooms
10. Navigation cabin
11. Chief of staff sea cabin
12. Admiral's bathroom
13. Fan space
14. X+Y predictor room

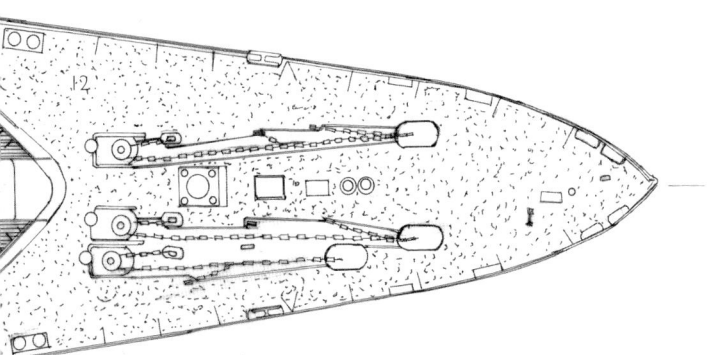

Vanguard: As-Completed Data

DATA AS COMPLETED

Built by John Brown, Clydebank.

Laid down:	2 October 1941.
Launched:	30 November 1944.
Completed:	for trials March 1946.
Commissioned:	25 April 1946.
Displacement:	45,116 tons light load, 51,420 tons deep.
Length:	759ft 11⅜in (pp), 799ft 11⅜in (wl), 814ft 4⅙in (oa).
Beam:	108ft.
Draught:	28ft 11in forward, 32ft 8in aft.
Freeboard (load condition):	36ft 8in forward, 23ft amidships, 25ft 6in aft.

Armament
8 x 15in 42cal Mk I RP12 (100rpg). In four twin turrets, all on centreline on upper deck, two forward and two aft, inner pair superfiring over outer mounts.

16 x 5.25in 50cal Mk I (391rpg). In eight twin turrets, four port and starboard on upper deck in two groups amidships, spaced well apart.

10 x 6-barrel 40mm Mk VI Bofors. Four on forward superstructure (two P + S), two abeam second funnel (P + S), three on after superstructure, one P + S on centreline and one on after end of superstructure, one on quarterdeck right aft.

1 x twin 40mm STAAG Bofors mount on top of 'B' 15in gun turret.

11 x 40mm Bofors single mounts. Two on forecastle abeam 'B' turret, four on after superstructure (P + S), five on quarterdeck, two abeam 'X' turret, three abaft Y' turret.

No TT.

Armour
(Vertical)
Main belt 14in with lower edge of 4½in
Main belt abreast machinery 13in
Armoured ends once outside citadel 13–12–11in
Bulkheads 12in
Turrets 13in faces, 9–7in sides, 10in rears and 6in roof
Barbettes 13in outer walls, 12–11in centre lines
Secondary casemates and shields 2½in
Splinter bulkheads fore and aft 1in
Funnel uptakes 1in
Cordite handing rooms 1in
Protection to rind bulkhead 2in
Conning tower 3in face, 2½in sides and rear.
Plotting office and tube 2in
DCT 2in
Cable trunks 2in

(Horizontal)
Main decks over magazines 6in
Main deck over machinery 5in
Lower deck forward of citadel 5–2½in
Lower deck aft 4–2in
Secondary turrets 2½in roofs
Magazines 1½in
Conning tower roof and floor 1–2in
Plotting office roof 1in
Superstructure protection 1in

Machinery
Engined by John Brown, Clydebank.
Parsons single-reduction geared turbines driving 4 screws.
Inner propellers 5-bladed, outer 3-bladed.
Boilers: 8 Admiralty 3-drum.
Designed SHP: 130,000 for 30 knots.
Sea speed: 29.75 knots.
Fuel: 4,897 tons oil plus 427 tons diesel and 200 tons in separate double bottom tanks.
Machinery in 4 units each watertight and self-contained. One unit comprised two separate watertight compartments.
Each engine room contained 2 main turbines driving a shaft through double helical gears at a working pressure of 350psi and temperature of 700°F.
Astern turbine was incorporated in the casing of the low pressure one.
Cruising turbines were in the original design but dropped later to save weight.
General Radius of Action: 7,560 miles @ 12 knots, 4,930 miles @ 24 knots, 3,560 miles @ 29 knots.
Tactical Diameter: 1,025 yards @ 30 knots, 935 yards @ 10 knots.
Time of turn 360 degrees 4 minutes 55 seconds.
Heel 4 degrees.
Rudder area 386ft.

Auxiliary Machinery
2 machinery rooms for harbour duties and 10 machinery rooms for general and action requirements.
4 diesel generators of 450KW, 2 forward of the machinery spaces and 2 abreast the after engine rooms.
4 turbo generators of 480KW located abreast the forward boiler rooms and 2 in the harbour machinery rooms between the forward engine rooms.
4 95hp motor-driven air compressors and 2 25hp compressors to supply free air where needed.
Four turbo pumps supplied the hydraulic pressure for the main armament.

Searchlights
4 x 20in, 2 port and starboard of bridge tower. Normal SL equipment was replaced by radar and only signalling SL were carried.

Costs
£11,530,503 which included £3,186,868 for armament but not including the original costs for the 15in guns and turrets.

Aircraft
None.

Complement
1,818 (1946)
1,935 (1951)
2,010 as Fleet Flagship (1946)
1,893 as private ship (1946)

Hull and Special Features

Vanguard was initially designed for a standard displacement of 42,500 tons corresponding to a draught of 28ft mean but these figures increased by 2,000 tons and 1ft respectively owing to several modifications in the design whilst under construction.

She was originally to have been about 7,500 tons heavier than the *King George V* class with an increase of 69ft 4in in length, 5ft beam and 4in on the mean draught, the increase in length obviously to accommodate the additional 15in gun turret. The displacement, as completed was about 5,000 tons heavier than the *King George V*s (as they were in 1945 after wartime additions)

Under an Admiralty requirements (in force prior to 1940) that all turrets should be able to fire their guns at 3 degrees depression over their entire safety arcs, the *King George V* class had only a very slight sheer forward with a vertical stem which proved very wet at high speeds or in a strong seaway. *Vanguard* was similar as designed but following sea experience with the *King George V*s, the forecastle sheer was greatly increased while building, with a raking stem and greater flare.

The flat stern, which had first appeared in the cruiser-minelayer *Adventure* as completed in 1926, was adopted for the first time in any British capital ship (also in the *Lion* design) in order to save weight and simplify construction. Other arguments advanced in favour of the flat stern, which was to become the standard pattern in the British and foreign navies, were that any hull structure above the rudder post merely created extra drag without adding anything in efficiency, while the stern wave, travelling faster than the hull itself, actually pushed against the flat section and thereby assisted speed.

With her straight-sided non-bulbous hull and recessed hawse pipes for her anchors flush with the hull *Vanguard* turned out to be a magnificent sea boat which proved to be dry and steady in the most severe of weather conditions.

Special features in general:

1. Flush-decked hull with a short steep sheer forward.
2. Bow flare much deeper than in preceding classes.
3. Three breakwaters fitted forward of 'A' turret.
4. Flat, square-cut stern.

Below: Finally leaving the John Brown shipyard, *Vanguard* is towed by tugs down the Clyde on 2 May 1946.

Left: As she comes down the Clyde on her first journey she is photographed extensively and shows her appearance to the public for the first time. The 14-mile trip took 2½ hours.

Passing along the banks of the Clyde, *Vanguard* is gazed upon by a mixture of young and old. The youngsters are amazed at such a massive warship so near to them and the older generation look across to her having seen many battleships pass before, maybe even the mighty *Hood* when she sailed down the same route some 26 years previously. What they probably did not realise was that they would never see another new battleship sail down the Clyde.

Having completed her first journey from the Clyde to the Tail of the Bank at Greenock, *Vanguard* is prepared for her first trials. This view of her was one of the first photographs to appear in *Jane's Fighting Ships* in the 1947 edition, specifically taken to show her flat stern.

HULL AND SPECIAL FEATURES

Right: An early Royal visit to the ship by HRH Princess Elizabeth to witness the ship's commissioning service on 12 May 1946. The Princess is seen here being greeted by Captain W G Agnew as she sets foot on the ship for the first time. For the ceremony the crew were mustered on the quarterdeck whilst the service was carried out by Archdeacon J K Wilson, Chaplain of the Fleet. The Princess also attended the dedication of the chapel on board and was later presented with a coloured engraving of the first HMS *Vanguard* of 1586.

VANGUARD STABILITY AND GM, 11 JUNE 1946

Average Action Condition
Displacement: 50,145 tons.
Fuel on board: 3,607 tons oil with 100 tons water protection and reserve feed tanks full.
Draught: 34ft 3in.
GM: 7.48ft.
Maximum stability: 34.5 degrees.
Vanishing point: 65.3 degrees.

Extreme Deep Condition
Displacement: 51,420 tons.
Fuel on board: 4,868 tons with 100 tons water protection and reserve feed tanks full.
Draught: 35ft.
GM: 8.20ft.
Maximum stability: 35 degrees.
Vanishing point: 68 degrees.

Light Load Condition
Displacement: 45,116 tons.
No fuel, water or provisions.
Draught: Ship lightened to 31ft 2in.
GM: 5.89ft.
Maximum stability: 35 degrees.
Vanishing point: 60.7 degrees.

5. Boats stowed on two levels, amidships between the two funnels and handled by aircraft-type cranes but without the quick-snatch hoist required to jerk planes off the top of a wave.
6. Accommodation was especially well planned and included five dining halls, a chapel and for the first time in a British warship a cinema was installed.
7. Completely enclosed messes provided for nearly all ratings.
8. Ventilation and refrigeration equipment was excellent.
9. Electric galleys and bakeries were the largest and best-equipped ever to be fitted to a British warship to that date and well up to American standards.
10. Air-conditioning in certain compartments fitted for tropical and Arctic conditions.
11. Action Information Centre which included an air plotting room, radar display room and operations room.
12. Habitability. The latest equipment was installed including bathrooms, stainless steel equipment, new furniture, water coolers, ice cream machine, electric deck scrubbers and polishers, electric washing machines, a modern laundry and a large barber shop.
13. Improved damage-control systems in place (isolation valves in better positions, extra pumps and dynamos for back-up to main machinery power in the event of damage etc).

HULL AND SPECIAL FEATURES

The first set of photographs taken on board were mainly posed views showing crew carrying out various tasks. Note that in this one of her forecastle and bridge, the radar aerials have been deleted. There were some publications, even at that early stage (1946) that was suggesting that her use was simply as an escort for aircraft carriers and asking if battleships were really necessary in the post-war fleet. The opposite view was that as she rested at anchor on the sunlit waters of the Firth she represented the epitome of naval power and strength.

Armament

All three final designs for the new battleship were based on them being armed with eight 15in guns which were to be mounted in the four turrets which had been removed from the old battlecruisers *Glorious* and *Courageous* when they were both reconstructed as aircraft carriers in the 1920s.

It was obvious that the turrets would have to be modernised to enhance their potential and bring them up to date and suitable for wartime conditions in the 1940s. The 15in gun turrets that had already been given an update were those in the old battleships *Queen Elizabeth*, *Valiant* and the battlecruiser *Renown* when those ships were completely reconstructed before the Second World War. These were generally viewed as a success and it was only natural that any new construction with 15in guns and turrets would proceed along the same lines.

This task was given to the shipyard of Harland and Wolff, the same yard that had originally built HMS *Glorious* in 1916. The priority was to enhance the turrets' protection and their whole structure was given much thicker plates (see armour layout). The gun ports were cut away to allow for increased elevation and the guns were given pneumatic run-out. Internally the turrets were completely modernised. Other modifications were the elimination of any weak points and a revamping of the revolving structure to bring them into line with modern requirements.

Fitting *Vanguard*'s main armament proved no easy task owing to the fact that the turrets and mountings were originally constructed for *Glorious* and *Courageous* which had the magazines above the shell rooms but, as history had proved, the reverse was the best method to enhance protection for the magazines by placing them under the shell rooms as was done in *Nelson*, *Rodney* and the *King George V* class. Many extra anti-flash precautions were included in the new mounts with the handing rooms being above the shell rooms and flash-tight doors being fitted where possible. The original 15ft rangefinders were replaced with new 30ft ones. As completed the result was very similar to that of the 15in IN mounting as fitted in *Queen Elizabeth* etc but the magazines, shell rooms, handing rooms and embarking arrangements in *Vanguard* were of an improved design over those early conversions.

The new turrets were fitted with remote power control (RPC) training gear which involved the redesign of many valves, pointer drives and wheel gearing. Further improvements were:

1. Turret ventilation with larger fans fitted and heaters to condition the air in cold climates.
2. A circular path of rollers was fitted around the trunk to assist in the transfer of cordite from the fixed to the revolving structure.
3. Special fittings to the gun ports and barbettes against weather.

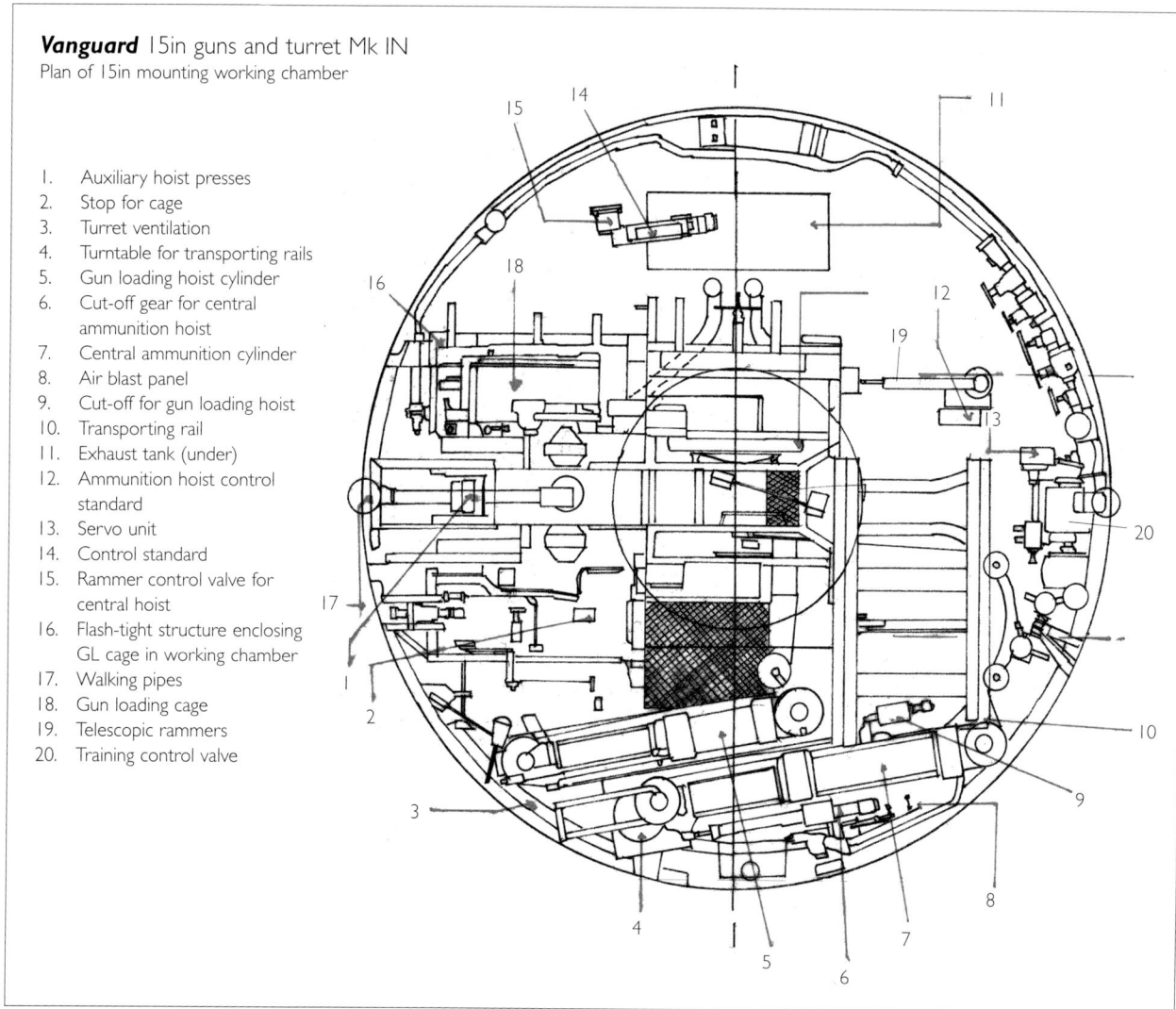

Vanguard 15in guns and turret Mk IN
Plan of 15in mounting working chamber

1. Auxiliary hoist presses
2. Stop for cage
3. Turret ventilation
4. Turntable for transporting rails
5. Gun loading hoist cylinder
6. Cut-off gear for central ammunition hoist
7. Central ammunition cylinder
8. Air blast panel
9. Cut-off for gun loading hoist
10. Transporting rail
11. Exhaust tank (under)
12. Ammunition hoist control standard
13. Servo unit
14. Control standard
15. Rammer control valve for central hoist
16. Flash-tight structure enclosing GL cage in working chamber
17. Walking pipes
18. Gun loading cage
19. Telescopic rammers
20. Training control valve

ARMAMENT

Vanguard 15in guns and turret Mk IN
General arrangement of mounting – side elevation, 1946

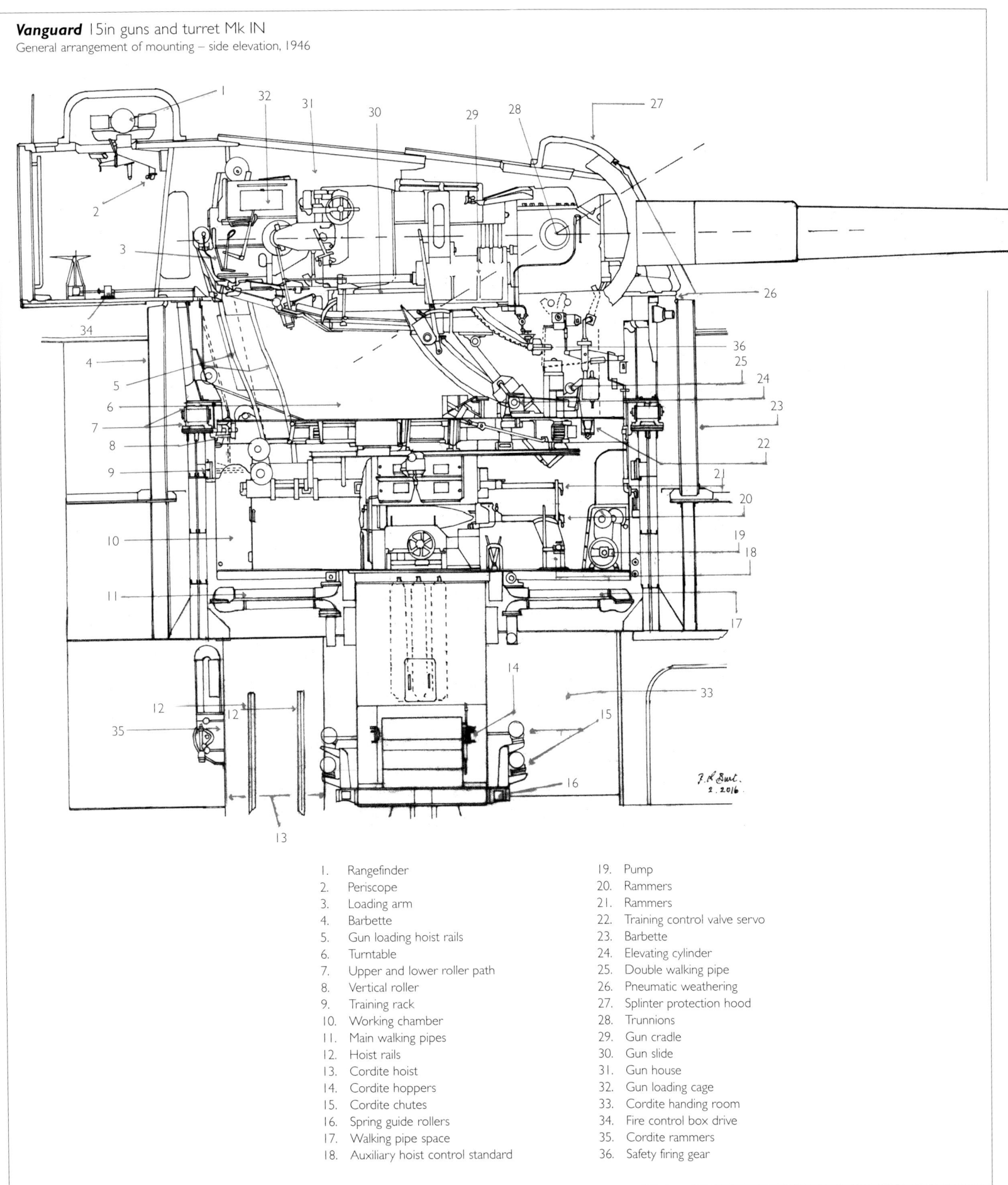

1. Rangefinder
2. Periscope
3. Loading arm
4. Barbette
5. Gun loading hoist rails
6. Turntable
7. Upper and lower roller path
8. Vertical roller
9. Training rack
10. Working chamber
11. Main walking pipes
12. Hoist rails
13. Cordite hoist
14. Cordite hoppers
15. Cordite chutes
16. Spring guide rollers
17. Walking pipe space
18. Auxiliary hoist control standard
19. Pump
20. Rammers
21. Rammers
22. Training control valve servo
23. Barbette
24. Elevating cylinder
25. Double walking pipe
26. Pneumatic weathering
27. Splinter protection hood
28. Trunnions
29. Gun cradle
30. Gun slide
31. Gun house
32. Gun loading cage
33. Cordite handing room
34. Fire control box drive
35. Cordite rammers
36. Safety firing gear

15in 42cal Mk IN GUN

Muzzle velocity:	2,400ft/sec.
Weight of shell:	1,920lbs (4CRH), 1,920lbs (6CRH) (there was also an improved shell of 1,938lb).
Weight of charge:	430lbs.
Recoil of gun with full charge:	46in.
Elevation/depression:	+30 degrees/-4½ degrees.
Speed of elevation:	5 degrees per second.
Range:	33,000–36,500yds at maximum elevation and depending on charge used.

4. Air blast gear, electrical boxes, elevation machinery, new shell bogie equipment and further improvements to cordite handling owing to the fact that the magazines were now fitted below the shell rooms.

The 15in guns used in *Vanguard* were spares that had been used before in the *Royal Sovereign* and *Queen Elizabeth* classes, which were made of steel and wire construction and consisted of an inner A tube, B tube, jacket shrunk collar, breech ring, breech bush and wire with stop and filling rings. The gun was interchangeable for use in right or left positions within the turret. The breech mechanism was of the interrupted stepped-screw type mounted on a swinging carrier, the latter being hinged to lugs on the frame of the breech mechanism. It could also be operated by a handwheel mounted on the frame slightly forward of the upper lug.

The weight of the gun on its own was 97 tons 3cwt on its own and 100 tons with the breech mechanism fitted. The total revolving weight of the turret including shell room and associated machinery was 904 tons.

The mounting consisted of a gun house, working chamber and main trunk. The main trunk extended down to the shell handing room, passing through various levels and then the magazines were placed below. The shells and cordite were lifted up to the main trunk in main cages which were in two parts, one for the shell and one for the cordite. The shells were loaded into the main cage from a revolving shell bogie capable of being clutched either to the trunk or to the fixed structure of the ship.

Vanguard's newly-refurbished main armament turned out to be very successful but some felt that it had been a poor compromise and even said it was obsolete. It was pointed out at the time, however, that the turrets and guns even in their original condition were well tested in action and reliable, and the new version had an improved range and rate of fire, good hitting power and although not quite the same punch as a 16in gun they were to prove throughout their service history to be one of the best and most successful heavy guns fitted aboard any capital ship in the Royal Navy. In May 1946 the first gun trials were carried out and twenty-four full broadsides were fired from the 15in guns and twenty-three broadsides from the 5.25in. The 40mm Bofors guns were also tested and in general the trials were a complete success as far as armament was concerned.

The 5.25in Mk I dual-purpose secondary armament, controlled by four US Mk 37 directors arranged in a diamond formation, was chosen for *Vanguard* as these guns and their equipment had already been mounted in the *King George V* class and had a reasonable weight of shell which could be loaded by an

Vanguard
15in gun breech Mk I mechanism (closed), 1946

1. Hand wheel
2. Rack
3. Air blast pipe
4. Hydraulic cylinder
5. Breech safety contacts
6. Catch retaining breech screw closed
7. Breech screw
8. Carrier
9. Air blast
10. Lock bolts

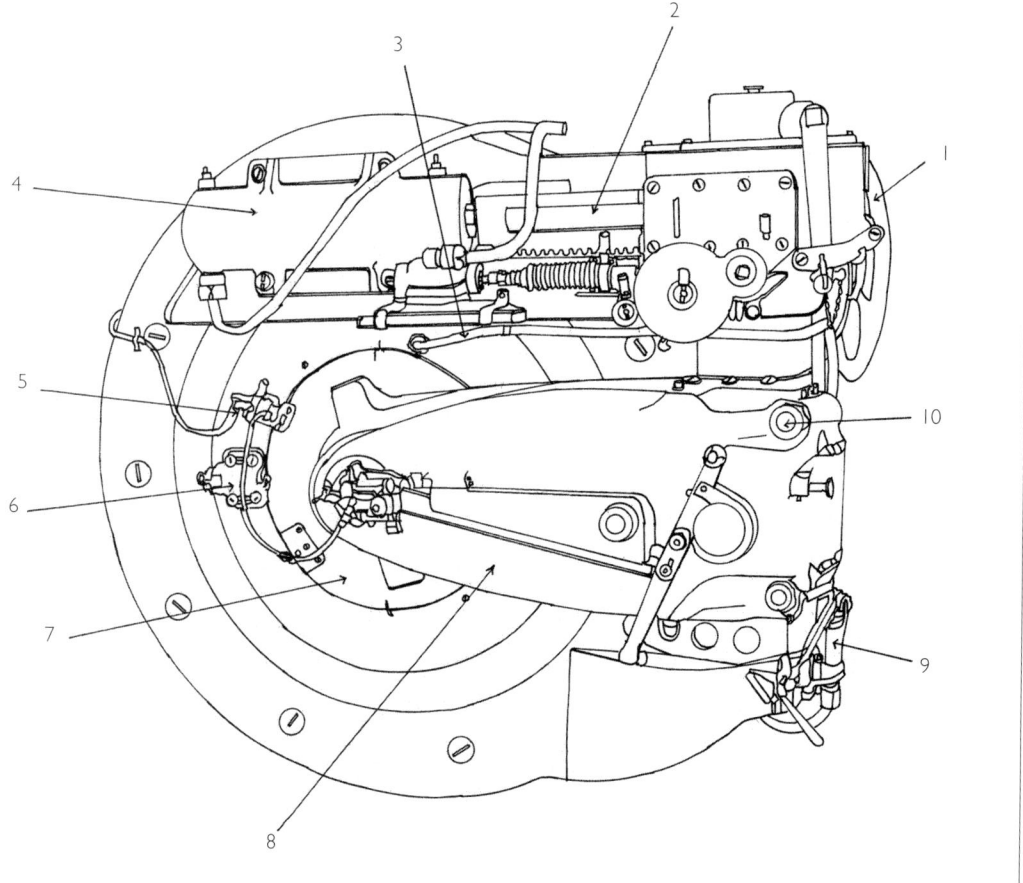

ARMAMENT

Vanguard
15in modified gun turret – rear elevation, 1946

1. Gun house
2. Elevation receiver
3. Chain rammer
4. Gun loading hoist exhaust tank
5. Elevating cylinder
6. Shell grab
7. Turret buffer
8. Walking pipe space
9. Cordite handing room
10. Cordite chutes
11. Shell bogie
12. Flash door
13. Air blast pivot
14. Magazine
15. Conveyor
16. Door for access to air bottles
17. Cordite hoist
18. Shell handing room
19. Hopper
20. Hoist winch
21. Exhaust tank
22. Training rack and pinion
23. Turntable rollers
24. Lifting jacks
25. Gun loading cage
26. Training gear
27. Clutch lever
28. Elevating hand wheel
29. Elevation receiver
30. Breech mechanism
31. Training hand wheel

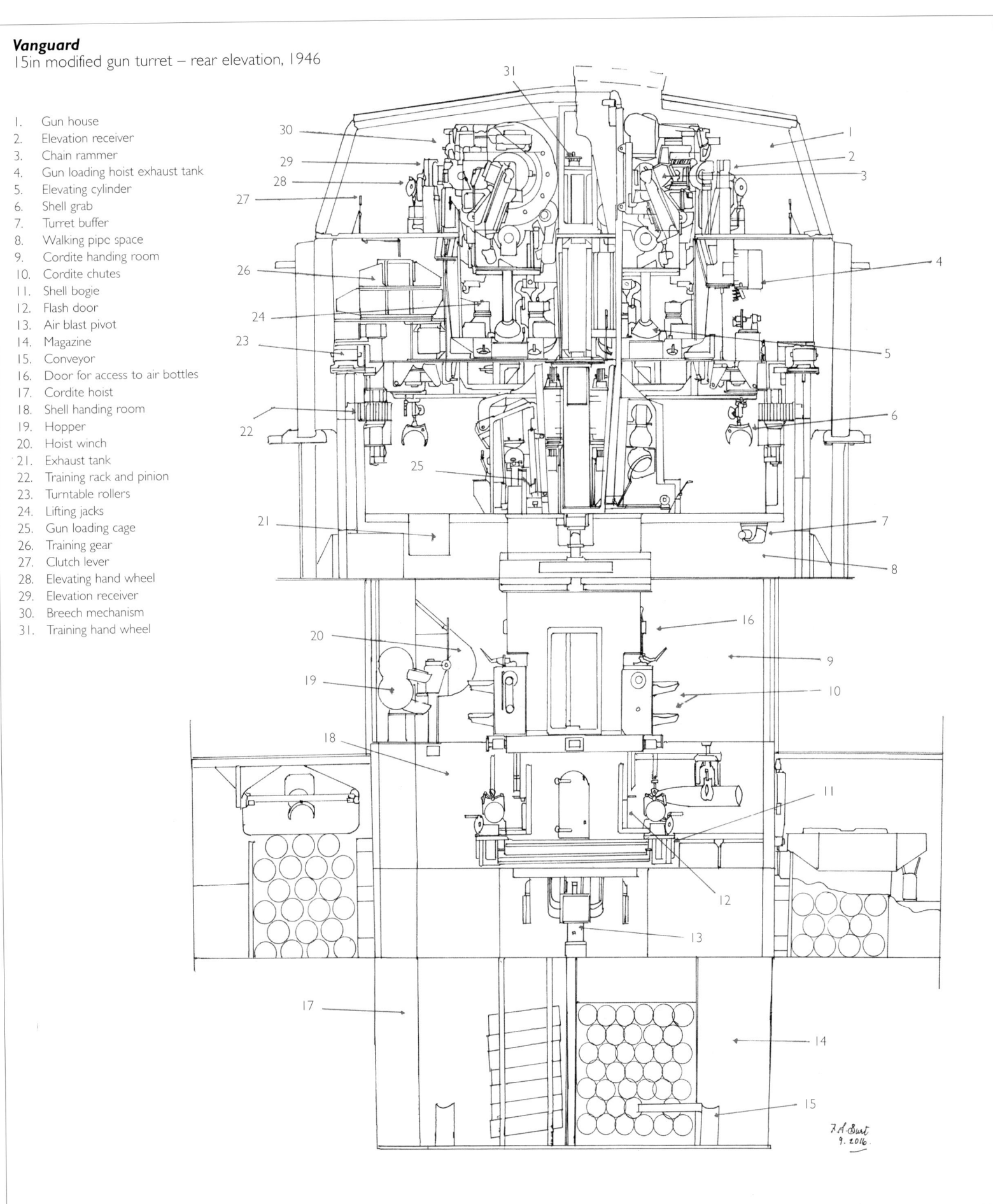

average crew who it was hoped could sustain a long period of ammunition flow at all elevations without too much fatigue. On paper the rate of fire was ten to twelve rounds per gun per minute.

The Mk I 5.25in mount was fitted with a short trunk which was given a D quality 1in shield. The short mounting rather than the longer mounting in the Mk II was fitted in *Vanguard* because it proved impracticable to fit long mountings vertically above the magazines. The turret was slightly modified and fitted with RP10 control.

The guns were of all-steel construction consisting of loose barrel, jacket, removable breech ring and sealing collar. The barrel was rifled on the Polygroove system with 36 grooves having a uniform twist of one turn in 30 calibres. The length of the bore was 50 calibre (21ft 10½in)

During the Second World War battleships of all nations had their anti-aircraft batteries increased because of the need to repel constant attacks by enemy aircraft. With displacement increases being ignored, the battleships of the Royal Navy old and new were fitted with extra anti-aircraft guns wherever they could be placed. Wartime experience, however, showed that attacks from aircraft were proving more than problematic owing to the fact that they were bombing or torpedoing ships with little or no concern for the constant barrage of anti-aircraft fire. When HMS *Prince of Wales* and *Repulse* were sunk in December 1941 it was officially recorded:

> 11.18 hours 1 hit on *Repulse* – no serious damage.
> 11.44 hours 1 probably 2 hits on *Prince of Wales*.
>   Ship listed 11½ degrees to port.
> 11.56 hours *Repulse* avoids 3 torpedoes.
> 11.58 hours Attack on *Repulse* … no hits.
> 12.22 hours 1 hit on *Repulse* port side;
>   3 to 4 hits on *Prince of Wales* starboard side.
> 12.25 hours 4 hits on *Repulse*: sank 12.33 hours
> 12.44 hours 1 hit on *Prince of Wales*: sank 13.20 hours.

'Enemy was in no way perturbed by our gunfire!' The sinking of

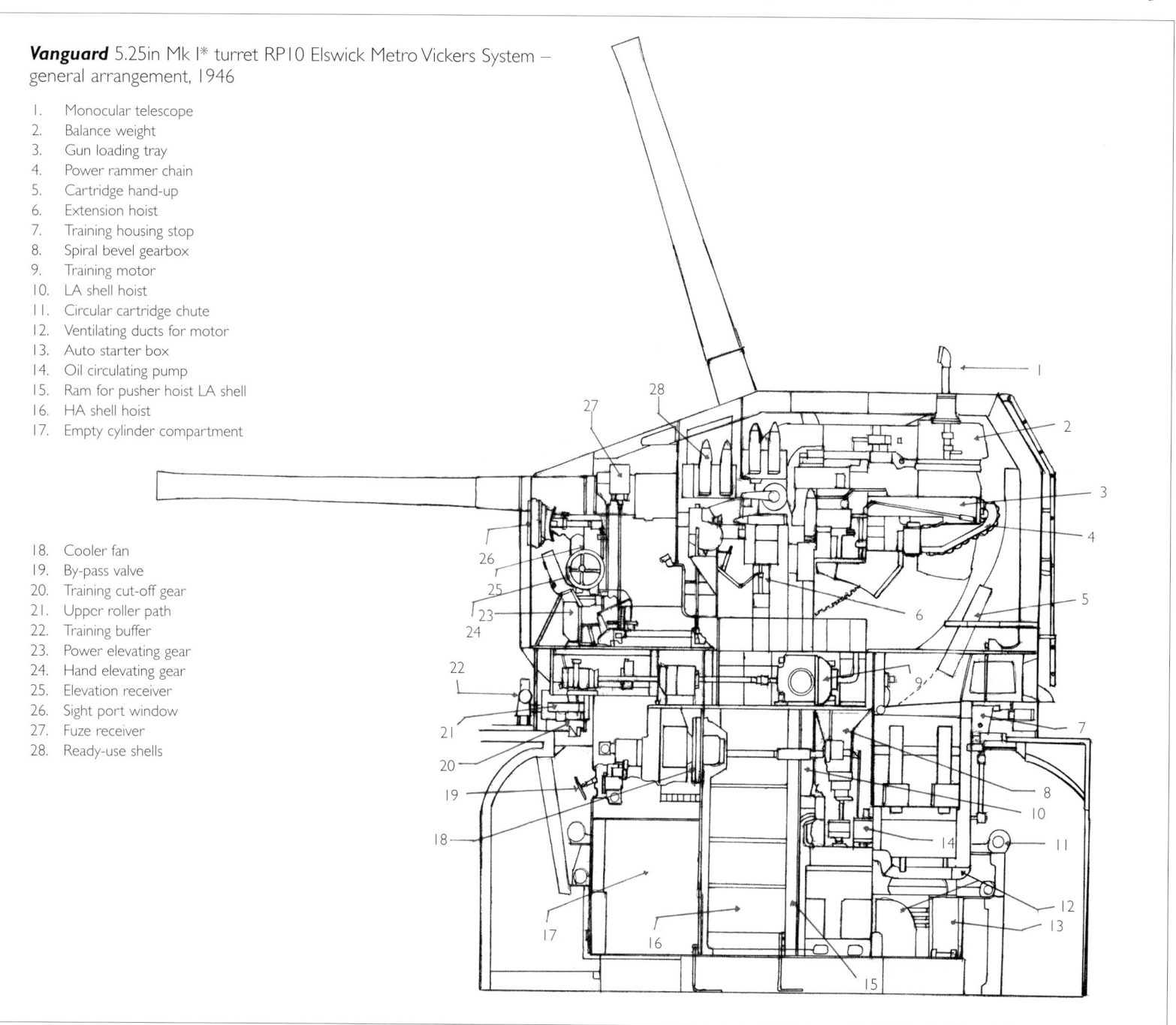

Vanguard 5.25in Mk I* turret RP10 Elswick Metro Vickers System – general arrangement, 1946

1. Monocular telescope
2. Balance weight
3. Gun loading tray
4. Power rammer chain
5. Cartridge hand-up
6. Extension hoist
7. Training housing stop
8. Spiral bevel gearbox
9. Training motor
10. LA shell hoist
11. Circular cartridge chute
12. Ventilating ducts for motor
13. Auto starter box
14. Oil circulating pump
15. Ram for pusher hoist LA shell
16. HA shell hoist
17. Empty cylinder compartment
18. Cooler fan
19. By-pass valve
20. Training cut-off gear
21. Upper roller path
22. Training buffer
23. Power elevating gear
24. Hand elevating gear
25. Elevation receiver
26. Sight port window
27. Fuze receiver
28. Ready-use shells

ARMAMENT

5.25in Mk I GUN

Weight of gun and mechanism:	4 tons 6cwt.
Weight of sighting gear:	12 cwt.
Weight of gun house and shield incl. support and platform:	7 tons.
Distance between guns:	96in.
Muzzle velocity:	2,690ft/sec.
Weight of shell:	80lbs.
Weight of charge:	18.6lbs.
Recoil on firing:	24in.
Elevation/depression:	+70 degrees/ -5 degrees.
Range:	23,400– 24,000 yds.
Rate of fire:	7 to 8 rounds per gun per minute (although official early records states 10 to 12).

these two major warships and the fact that their AA defence had little or no effect on the incoming attacks sent shockwaves through both the Admiralty departments and the Government alike. Although the sinking became general knowledge, this document was not released to the public until March 1955.

During the construction of *Vanguard* and up to the end of the Second World War all of the front-line British battleships had been overloaded with numerous additional AA guns as defence against air attack had become as important to a battleship's safety as her main underwater protection. In 1943 a statement by the Admiralty reflected this line of thought:

> Before the present stage of the development of aircraft was reached the gun was the main offensive weapon of a fleet and armour its main protection against the main enemy attack by gunfire. Aircraft development has now so radically altered this that the main offensive weapon, which was the gun, is now the aircraft; and the main protection against the enemy's main

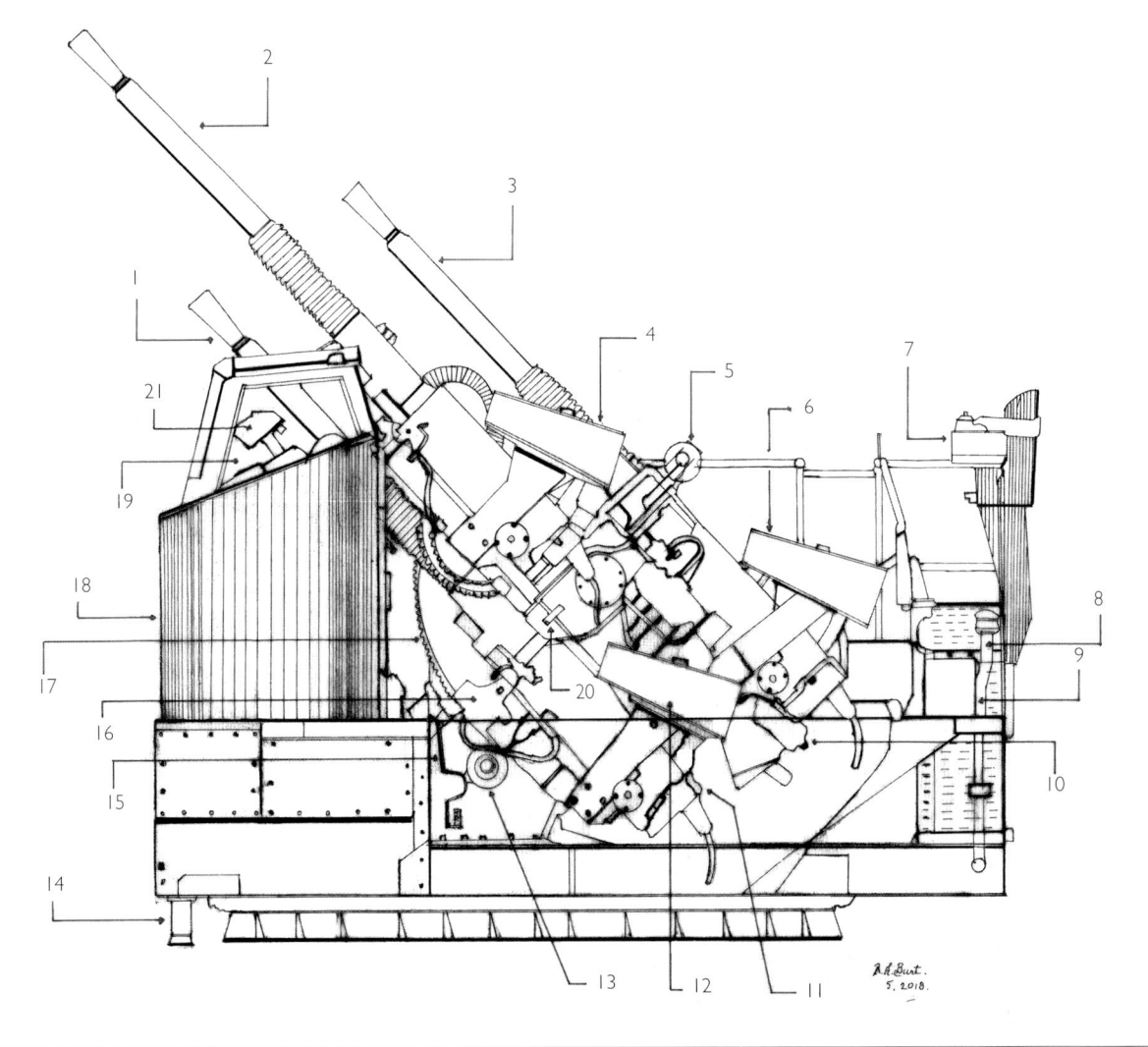

Mk VI 6-barrel 40mm Bofors mount, 1946
General arrangement, left hand elevation

1. No 6 gun (1–3+5 on right hand side)
2. No 4 gun
3. No 2 gun
4. Ammunition feed tray (24rpg)
5. Firing gear oil tank
6. Ammunition feed tray (36rpg)
7. Captain of the mounting's seat
8. Firing solenoid
9. Cooling water
10. Accumulator
11. Re-cocking lever
12. Ammunition feed tray (24rpg)
13. Left-hand elevating pinion
14. Training housing stop
15. Safety firing gear
16. Left-hand firing gear pump
17. Elevating arc
18. Control cabin
19. Window
20. Firing cylinder
21. Sights

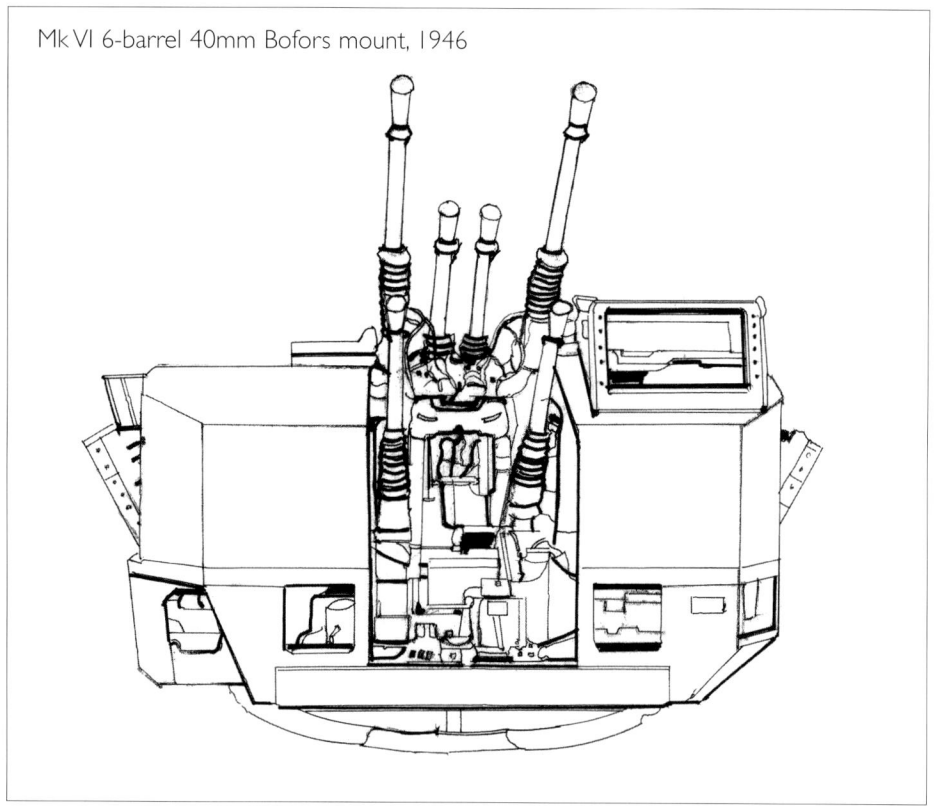

Mk VI 6-barrel 40mm Bofors mount, 1946

weapon, which was armour, has now become the fighter aircraft, coupled with efficient A/A armament and underwater protection.

The 2pdr pom-poms and 20mm cannon fitted to most ships did not seem to provide an effective deterrent against attacking aircraft and the need for improvement was a serious issue. During the war a new type of single-barrel 40mm Bofors gun had been developed which needed only one man to operate it. This single mount was found to be quite successful and was later given twin barrels with the addition of radar in the form of the Type 282 aerial but this could only be used for ranging and the mount was only capable of visual fire. This was the Mk I STAAG.

Further development saw the twin-barrel Mk II mount (at first called Simple Tachymetric Anti-Aircraft Gun then officially called Stabilised Tachymetric Gun) which was fitted with Type 262 radar as part of its integral fire-control system. Not only could it find the range but it could also control the gun in blind-fire conditions and was self-contained.

The 40mm STAAG Mk II was capable of 120 rounds per minute with a high effect shell with direct action fuses. The radar searched over an arc of 25 degrees centred on the bearing of the mount and up to 80 degrees of the angle of sight. The search was done by the radar aerial moving independently of the mount.

1. The effective range was 2,500 yards.
2. The weight of the mount was approximately 17½ tons
3. The mount was self-contained for power with provision for secondary arrangements for electrical back-up which enabled the mount to carry on firing if damaged as long as ammunition was supplied even if the ship was listing.
4. Stabilisation with only one gyro in use to give level of equipment, pitch, yaw and any alteration of the ship's course.
5. Prediction for any diving target was automatically calculated.
6 Radar auto-ranging system which obviated human error with any target signal automatically passing the range to the calculating system.
7. Radar auto-searching facilities which meant that the system could search and lock on to a target after receiving information from the indicator in the radar set.

These newly-developed 40mm mounts were worked into the design of any new construction where possible and *Vanguard* was one of them.

The original AA armament approved for *Vanguard* by 1945 saw great anxiety in the quest to fit her with a suitable up-to-date AA outfit but at that date the following was sanctioned until further notice.

10x 40mm (six-barrel).
1 x 40mm STAAG (twin-barrel).
6 x 20mm (quadruple).
14 x 20mm (single).

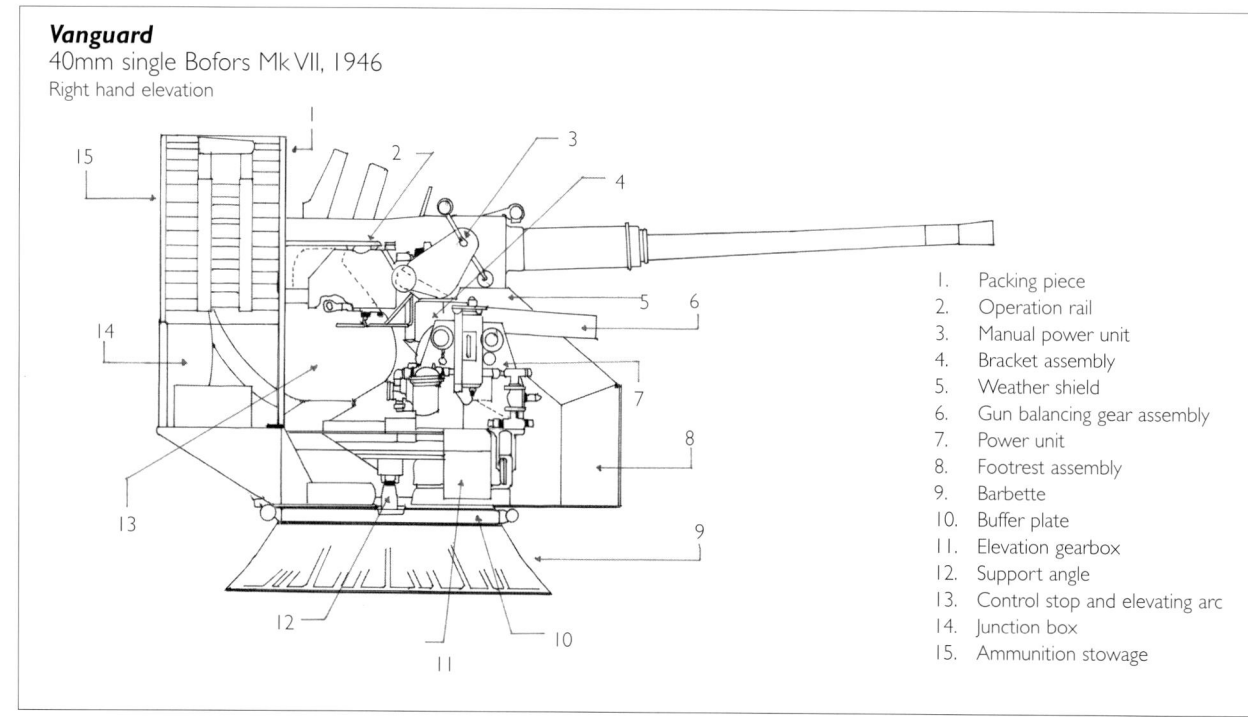

Vanguard
40mm single Bofors Mk VII, 1946
Right hand elevation

1. Packing piece
2. Operation rail
3. Manual power unit
4. Bracket assembly
5. Weather shield
6. Gun balancing gear assembly
7. Power unit
8. Footrest assembly
9. Barbette
10. Buffer plate
11. Elevation gearbox
12. Support angle
13. Control stop and elevating arc
14. Junction box
15. Ammunition stowage

ARMAMENT

STAAG Mk II 40mm twin Bofors (Type 262 RDF)
Self-training anti-aircraft gun or tachymetric AA gun

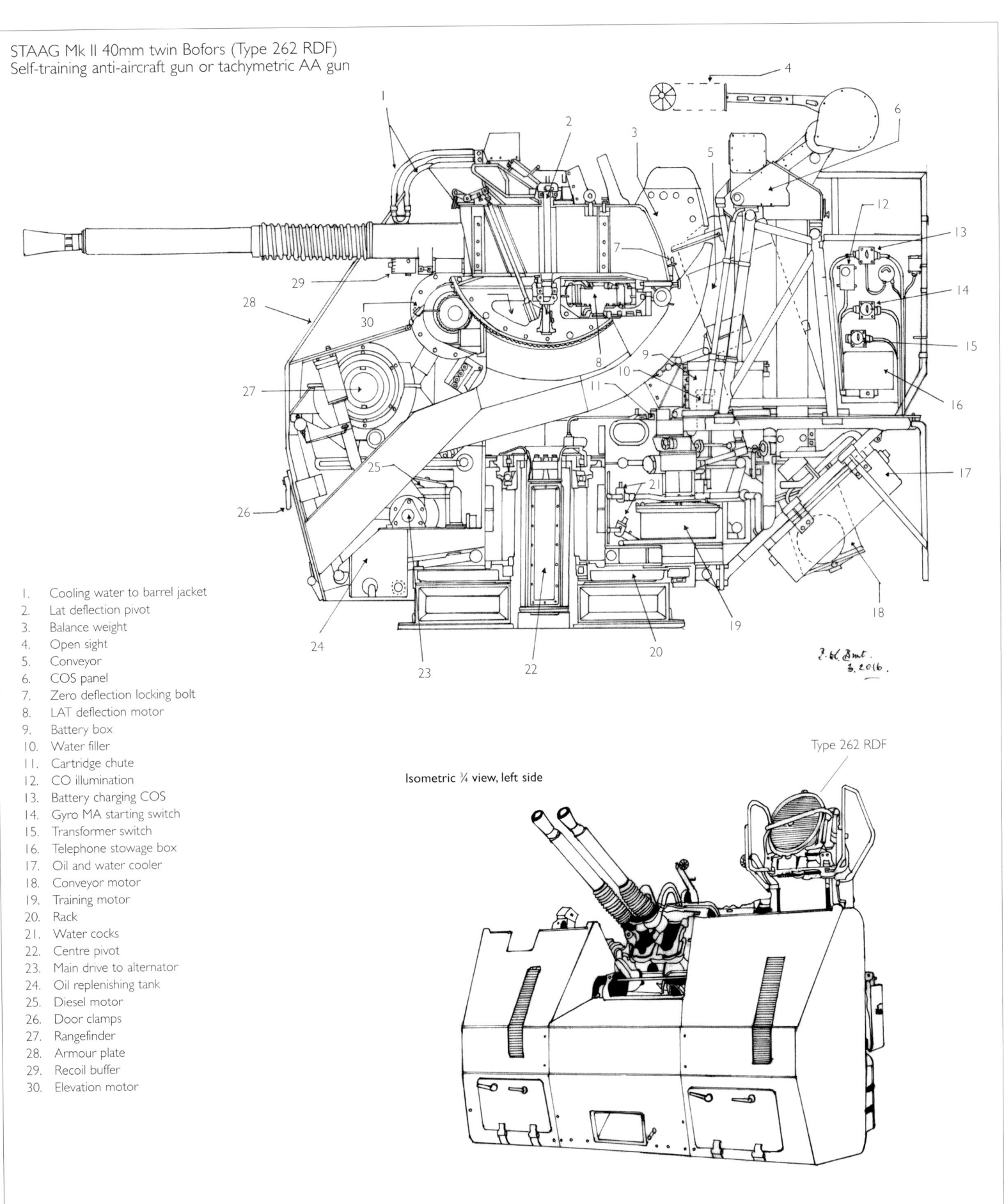

1. Cooling water to barrel jacket
2. Lat deflection pivot
3. Balance weight
4. Open sight
5. Conveyor
6. COS panel
7. Zero deflection locking bolt
8. LAT deflection motor
9. Battery box
10. Water filler
11. Cartridge chute
12. CO illumination
13. Battery charging COS
14. Gyro MA starting switch
15. Transformer switch
16. Telephone stowage box
17. Oil and water cooler
18. Conveyor motor
19. Training motor
20. Rack
21. Water cocks
22. Centre pivot
23. Main drive to alternator
24. Oil replenishing tank
25. Diesel motor
26. Door clamps
27. Rangefinder
28. Armour plate
29. Recoil buffer
30. Elevation motor

Isometric ¾ view, left side

Type 262 RDF

Right: Close-up of the aft 15in guns and turrets. Note the extensions to the gun ports to allow extra elevation. There are no blast bags but the guns have enclosed casings for the first time in a British 15in turret mount. Also note the single 40mm Bofors guns on the aft bridge and the six-barrel 40mm mounts visible just above.

By the end of the war, however, and with more experience from the fighting in the Far East which saw accurate air attack on ships on the increase, the 20mm mounts were dropped in favour of the heavier, harder-hitting 40mm mount and *Vanguard* was given eleven extra single 40mm single Bofors, making a total of seventy-three 40mm barrels. (See *Vanguard*'s final AA outfit in General data table.)

When the alteration from 20mm was made, it proved a problem with magazine storage and more space was needed for the larger and more numerous shells for the six-barrel 40mm mounts. A rearrangement of the magazines and general storage spaces was necessary but although this remedied the situation *Vanguard* never carried the full rounds per gun that she should have (1,564 rounds per barrel was the standard allowance but she ended up with only 1,269)

The twin mount and the six-barrel mount as fitted to *Vanguard* were the first of their type given to a British battleship and proved to be extremely accurate and far-ranging.

Mk VI BOFORS MOUNT AND GUN

Length of barrel:	88.75in.
Diameter of bore:	1.5748in.
Weight of barrel:	3½ cwt.
Weight of six guns with buffers filled but with no water in jackets:	2 tons 16 cwt.
Total weight of mount fully loaded:	21 tons 4cwt.
Length of barrel:	88.75in.
Diameter of bore:	1.5748in.
Muzzle velocity:	2,800ft/sec.
Recoil on firing:	8in.
Elevation/depression:	+90 degrees/-15 degrees.
Extreme range:	12,500 yards.

The six-barrel mount fitted in *Vanguard* was a far cry from the prototype conceived in January 1943. The original mount was completely enclosed, blastproof, weatherproof and had six mechanical hoists fed from outside the gun house. The weight of this mount and the limitation on a ship's displacement, however, demanded drastic reductions in size and weight and the early version was discarded. Further development produced a smaller unit, with firing, elevation and training all electrically controlled. The loading arrangements were altered to suit certain requirements depending on where the mounts were to be fitted, primarily for battleships and aircraft carriers.

The six-barrel mount in *Vanguard* was designated the Mk VI and was water cooled and fired HE shells at a rate of 120rpm up to a maximum of 60 degrees elevation which were self-destroying at 3,000 yards. The mount was auto-operated and could be used for both blind and visual fire as it was coupled to the Close Range Blind Fire (CRBF) director which was fitted with Type 262 radar.

The effective range was 2,500 yards and each of the guns was fitted with automatic feed trays with a capacity of six and nine clips (twenty-four and thirty-six rounds). The guns themselves were fitted on a saddle-like cradle – those on the right-hand side were numbered 1, 3 and 5, whilst those on the left were 2, 4 and 6 – and were cooled by water circulating through jackets at a rate of 6⅔ gallons per minute. The saddle-shaped cradle was mounted on the trunnions of a steel carriage which rotated on roller bearings.

Each mount was connected to an all-electric RP50 metadyne generator system so that elevating and training could be automatically controlled from the director. Hand operation of the mount was for maintenance only.

As completed in 1946, *Vanguard* carried one of the best and most sophisticated AA systems ever fitted in a British battleship.

Armour

Having worked for so long on a suitable armour layout for the new battleships of the 1936 Estimates (the *King George V* class), the considerable test results (from Job 74) favoured a thick side belt with a single thick armour deck at main deck level over all vitals. It was considered that this scheme for new-construction ships (the *Lion* class) was the best that could be afforded on a given limited displacement. The following *Lion*-class battleships of 1938 were given an almost identical armour layout to the *King George V*s and it seemed only natural for the same scheme to be applied to any battleship which would follow soon afterwards.

In general, the armour belt applied to *Vanguard* as fitted was very similar to that of both the *King George V*s and the *Lion* design but with modifications; the main belt being reduced by 1in and 3in respectively to offset the increased area of the longer belt and extra gun turret. The internal subdivision was also similar to that of the *King George V*s with solid bulkheads between the main compartments, access to these being by vertical shafts and fitted with watertight doors in all cases.

The main belt extended to just beyond the outer faces of 'A' and 'Y' barbettes with the upper edge at main-deck level. It was 14in thick abreast the magazines and 13in abreast the machinery and boiler rooms before tapering down to 5½in and 4½in at the lower edge. Twelve-inch bulkheads closed the forward and aft extremities between the main and lower decks, then reduced to 10in. Before and abaft the citadel a shallow 2–2½in belt was fitted to prevent any loss of water plane due to splinter damage.

The main deck flat extended over the main side belt and was 6in and 5in over magazines and 5in over machinery and boiler room spaces. The lower deck at the ends had 5–2½ in forward and 4½–2in aft.

Barbettes were 13–12–11in (see armour layout). Turrets had 13in faces, 9–7in sides, roofs of 6in and 10in rears. The 5.25in turrets had 2½in sides with 1in roofs. Ammunition hoists were 6–2in. Magazines were 1½in, cordite handing rooms were 1in and protection to the ring bulkhead was 2in.

The funnel uptakes were protected by 1in plates and the conning tower or navigating platform was given 3in plates to the face and 2½in to the sides and rear. The plotting office and tube was 2in and the cable trunks 2in also.

The full weight of the ship's armour protection, including some mild steel protective plating, was 15,265 tons.

As completed *Vanguard*'s deck armour was considered to be proof against 15in shells outside 31,000 yards and 1,000lb bombs from 14,000ft. Her main side belt was proof against 15in shells outside 15,000 yards.

In the light of wartime experience, *Vanguard*'s internal structure was enhanced to protect against underwater explosions. Behind the main armour belt the hull consisted of three longitudinal series of compartments. Inboard was a protective bulkhead of two thicknesses (⅝in and ⅞in) and wing compartments outboard of this were 3ft 6in–6ft 1in and 5ft 5in amidships. Between stations 156 and 178 a fourth longitudinal bulkhead was provided to prevent water entering vital positions within the hull. This system was stated to be proof against 1,000lbs of TNT.

The main function of the protective bulkhead was to limit any damage and stem any serious flooding caused by bombs or torpedoes. The extra bulkhead behind the protective bulkhead was to further prevent water seepage that might pass through any weakened seams or rivet holes and perhaps enter the engine or boiler rooms (as happened during the torpedo hits and the loss of *Prince of Wales* in December 1941). The sandwich system fitted to *Vanguard* consisted of a centre compartment containing liquid with air spaces inboard and outboard which afforded maximum protection against the force of any explosion. There were also double bottom compartment tanks which could be flooded and provide limited protection against mines and could also be used for counter-flooding.

As completed in 1946, regardless of comparisons with other contemporary battleships abroad, the *Vanguard* was one of the best-protected battleships ever built.

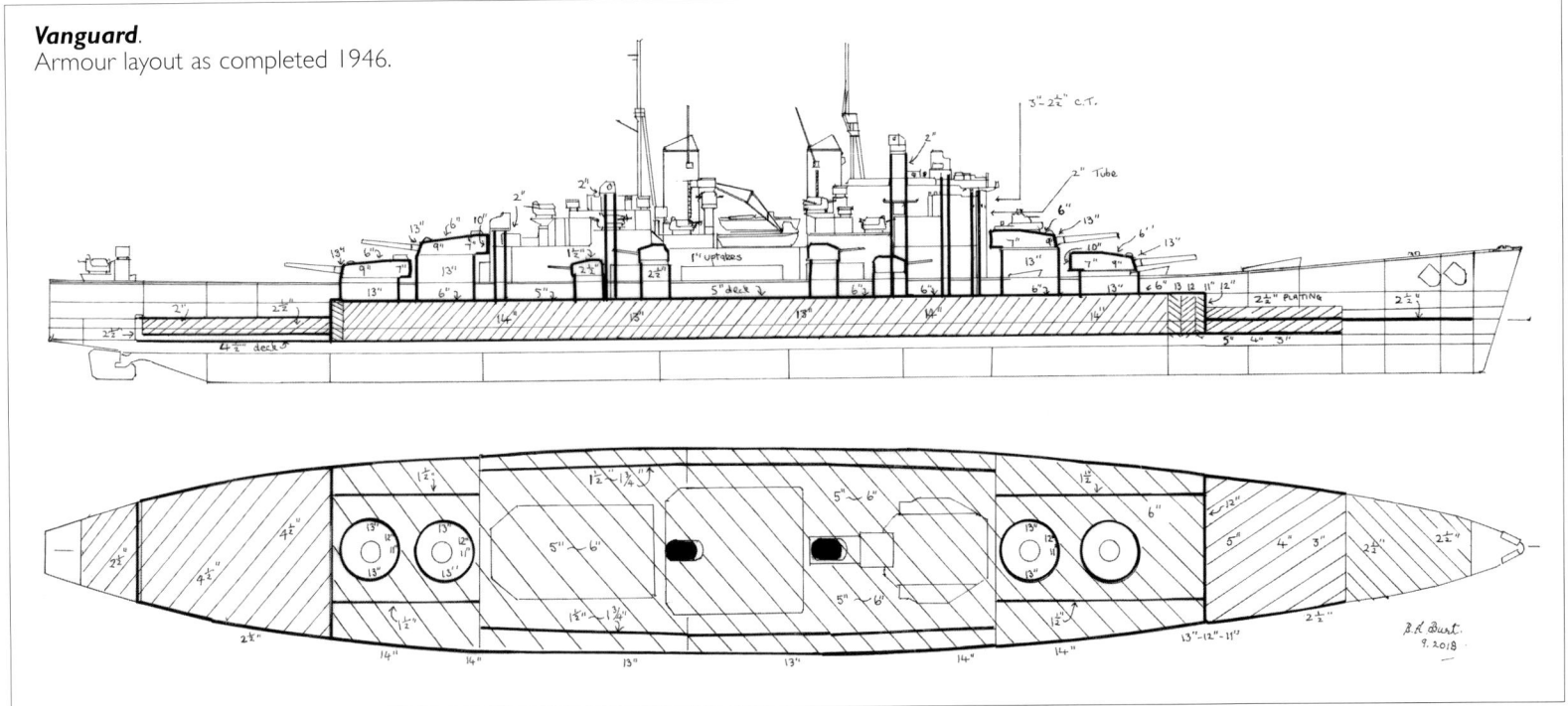

Vanguard. Armour layout as completed 1946.

Machinery

When the *King George V* class was being designed in 1936, there was much emphasis on producing a ship which would be considerably faster than existing British battleships. *Nelson* and *Rodney* completed in 1927 and were capable of 24 knots but this was seen as inadequate for new construction. France, Germany and Italy were all preparing ships which had speeds in excess of 28–29 knots. (France the *Dunkerques*, Germany the *Scharnhorst* and Italy the *Littorios*.)

Britain had faster capital ships in the three battlecruisers *Hood*, *Renown* and *Repulse* but a need for battleships to operate with them if necessary was an important requirement. With this in mind the machinery/boiler plant output for the *King George V* class was 110,000shp which gave them at least 28 knots. The machinery/boiler layout for the *Lion* class was very similar and *Vanguard* was also along the same lines with extra attention being paid to details regarding fittings and fixtures.

The main machinery in *Vanguard* consisted of four geared turbines capable of delivering 120,000shp which in fact actually produced over 130,000shp whilst on trials. The machinery was fitted in four units which could work separately under action conditions and were fitted with cross-connections for routine or emergency use. One unit comprised two separate watertight compartments.

Each engine room contained two main turbines driving a shaft through double helical gears at a working pressure of 350psi and a temperature of 700°F. Each turbine was capable of producing 30,000shp at approximately 245rpm. Astern turbines were incorporated into the low-pressure casing. Cruising turbines were a feature in the original design but were omitted at a later date to save weight.

Boiler rooms were arranged to carry two boilers of the Admiralty three-drum type with a working pressure of 400psi at a temperature of 250°F.

Vanguard's original electrical power plant was to consist of six turbo and two diesel generators which supplied a direct current at 220V into a ring main. As a result of wartime experience when in November 1939 the cruiser HMS *Belfast* set off a magnetic mine and the explosion caused her to lose all steam power, it was decided to increase the proportion of diesel generators in *Vanguard*. The final arrangement was four diesel generators of 450KW, two forward of the machinery spaces and two abreast the after engine rooms. There were also four turbo generators of 480KW fitted, two abreast the forward boiler rooms and two in the harbour machinery rooms near the engine rooms.

During her early steam trials a minor problem showed itself in the way of unwanted vibration from the machinery which was felt in certain areas of the ship especially in the engine rooms and in particular, the bridge itself. The aft CRBF director fitting at the extreme end of the quarterdeck was also affected. It was seen that when the ship manoeuvred or turned sharply when driving the shafts at over 180rpm the vibration was at its worst. As a result of this a temporary measure was imposed on her to avoid such moves until further tests were carried out. Investigations were to show that the original three-bladed propellers were partly to blame and these were duly replaced with five-bladed versions on the inner shafts with a stipulation that in future it was best to avoid sharp turning at high rpm on the shafts unless absolutely necessary.

During a refit in April 1951 slight bulging of the fire row tubes (A8–A15) of X1 boiler was observed. A further probe into the problem revealed that perforation of the tube had actually taken place. A full examination revealed that seven other A row tubes were found to be affected. The situation was rectified during the overhaul of the boilers, but it did show the problem of wear and tear in such high-pressure boiler equipment of such large capacity and output.

Below: A starboard broadside view of *Vanguard* whilst carrying out her turning trials in the Firth of Clyde off the Isle of Arran in June 1946. Note how tight her circle is for such a long ship (see notes on trials).

Left: As above. *Vanguard* on turning and manoeuvring trials. Note that the turrets are being worked at the same time.

Steam Trials, 11 July 1946

The steam trials that were carried out in *Vanguard* were exhaustive and being in peacetime they were executed over a rather lengthy period. Figures given in the Ship's Book are full sets but reduced to mean figures when inserted in the Ship's Cover.

Circle and Manoeuvring Trials, 1946

Continuing her lengthy trials *Vanguard* paced herself through circle and manoeuvring exercises throughout June and July 1946. The first of the manoeuvring tests were on 21 June and circle trials following on 7 and 8 July.

Bearing recorders were used to monitor her path with simultaneous measurements being taken of the ship's head, time of turn and speed of turns. The torque of the rudder was measured by

SHIP'S STEAM TRIALS MEAN FIGURES

Displacement	SHP	RPM	Speed
51,050 tons	6,130	91.8	11.860 knots
51,000 tons	12,640	118	15.266 knots
50,970 tons	24,110	146.6	18.963 knots
50,940 tons	31,360	159.5	20.557 knots
51,300 tons	38,240	170.3	21.873 knots
51,260 tons	64,960	201.6	25.477 knots
51,220 tons	75,120	210.8	26.285 knots
51,160 tons	102,240	230.9	28.160 knots
51,070 tons	132,950	250.6	30.379 knots

Boilers in use = 8   Water in each boiler = 7 tons 2cwt
Total capacity of water in main and reserve feed tanks = 428 tons

STEAM TRIALS

Six runs on the Arran course. At full power.

Mean of means on all shafts				Mean SHP			
'A'	'B'	'X'	'Y'	'A'	'B'	'X'	'Y'
250.5 revs	253	251.5	249	33,100	32,700	33,200	34,000 = 133,000
Second run							
252.5	252.5	249.5	249.5	33,800	32,600	33,300	33,600 = 133,300
Third run							
252	251	250	249	33,350	32,450	33,650	33,300 = 132,750
Fourth run							
252.5	252.5	250	249.5	33,600	32,600	33,300	33,600 = 133,100
Fifth run							
250	252.5	248	247	33,250	32,800	33,200	33,450 = 132,700
Sixth run							
251.3	255.5	248	249.5	33,400	33,000	32,900	33,800 = 133,100

Speeds obtained
1st run 30.252 knots
2nd run 30.457 knots
3rd run 30.252 knots
4th run 30.56 knots
5th run 30.201 knots
6th run 30.457 knots

Mean SHP on six runs = 132,992
Mean revolutions on six runs = 250.5568
Mean speed on six runs = 30.379 knots

PROPELLERS AS FITTED AT TIME OF TRIAL

	Starboard		Port	
Diameter	14ft 9in outer	14ft 9in inner	14ft 9in outer	14ft 9in inner
Pitch	14ft 8in outer	14ft 8in inner	14ft 8in outer	14ft 8in inner

electrical methods and instruments for recording heel, pitch and course were used during circle and all other trials.

It was stated that the heel recorder proved unsatisfactory and as the ship heeled a few degrees the instrument greatly exaggerated the heel and then when the ship did return to her normal angle the reading on the instrument did not return to normal. An attempt was made to use the ship's radar as a secondary method of plotting the ship's circles but again this was to prove unsatisfactory.

At the end of these trials it was shown that *Vanguard* met all expectations with figures closely resembling those that had been recorded for a test model of her.

The results gave *Vanguard* a tactical diameter of 1,025 yards at 30.8 knots, a quick response to small angles of rudder correction and good directional stability at all speeds.

Brief Summary of *Vanguard*'s Movements During Early Trials, 1946

Monday 17 June	Ship leaves Gladstone dock for steaming and vibration trials.
Tuesday 18 June	Anchored off the Tail of the Bank.
Wednesday 19 June	Steering and manoeuvring trials at sea.
Thursday 20 June	More steering trials.

Continued on page 62

ENDURANCE CALCULATIONS

Speed 10 knots	RPM 78	SHP 5,000	Fuel 6.2 tons	Endurance 7,160 miles
Speed 22 knots	RPM 176	SHP 40,000	Fuel 15 tons	Endurance 6,500 miles
Speed 29 knots	RPM 238	SHP 114,000	Fuel 30 tons	Endurance 3,750 miles

The above figures for radius of action reduced somewhat as the ship's bottom became dirty.

CIRCLE AND MANOUVERING TRIALS

Conditions of ship and weather.

21 June 1946	Displacement	45,350 tons		
5 July 1946	Displacement	46,640 tons	Sea Calm	Wind Force 1
6 July 1946	Displacement	46,550 tons.	Sea 3	Wind Force 6
7 July 1946	Displacement	46,450 tons.	Sea 3–4	Wind Force 6
8 July 1946	Displacement	46,230 tons	Sea 0	Wind Force 1

Circle trials at 15 knots were carried out on 5 July 1946.
Circle trials at 30.8 knots were carried out on 6 July 1946.
Circle trials at 25 knots were carried out on 7 July 1946.
Circle trials at 10 knots were carried out on 8 July 1946.

VANGUARD'S HANDLING COMPARED TO OTHER BATTLESHIPS

	Displacement	Speed	Rudder angle	Tactical diameter	Time of turn 360 degrees
Vanguard	41,600 tons	15 knots	35 degrees	940 yds	521 seconds
Howe	43,000 tons	14½ knots	35 degrees	927 yds	577 seconds
Rodney	37,250 tons	14 knots	34 degrees	670 yds	506 seconds
Renown	34,150 tons	15 knots	35 degrees	1,002 yds	685 seconds
Hood	40,900 tons	31 knots	35 degrees	1,240 yds	342 seconds
Royal Oak	31,250 tons	8¾ knots	35 degrees	512 yds	710 seconds
Warspite	31,564 tons	2 knots	35 degrees	458 yds	406 seconds
USS *Washington*	44,300 tons	14½ knots	35 degrees	565 yds	430 seconds

Right: A good clear view of *Vanguard*'s forecastle and bridge, December 1946.

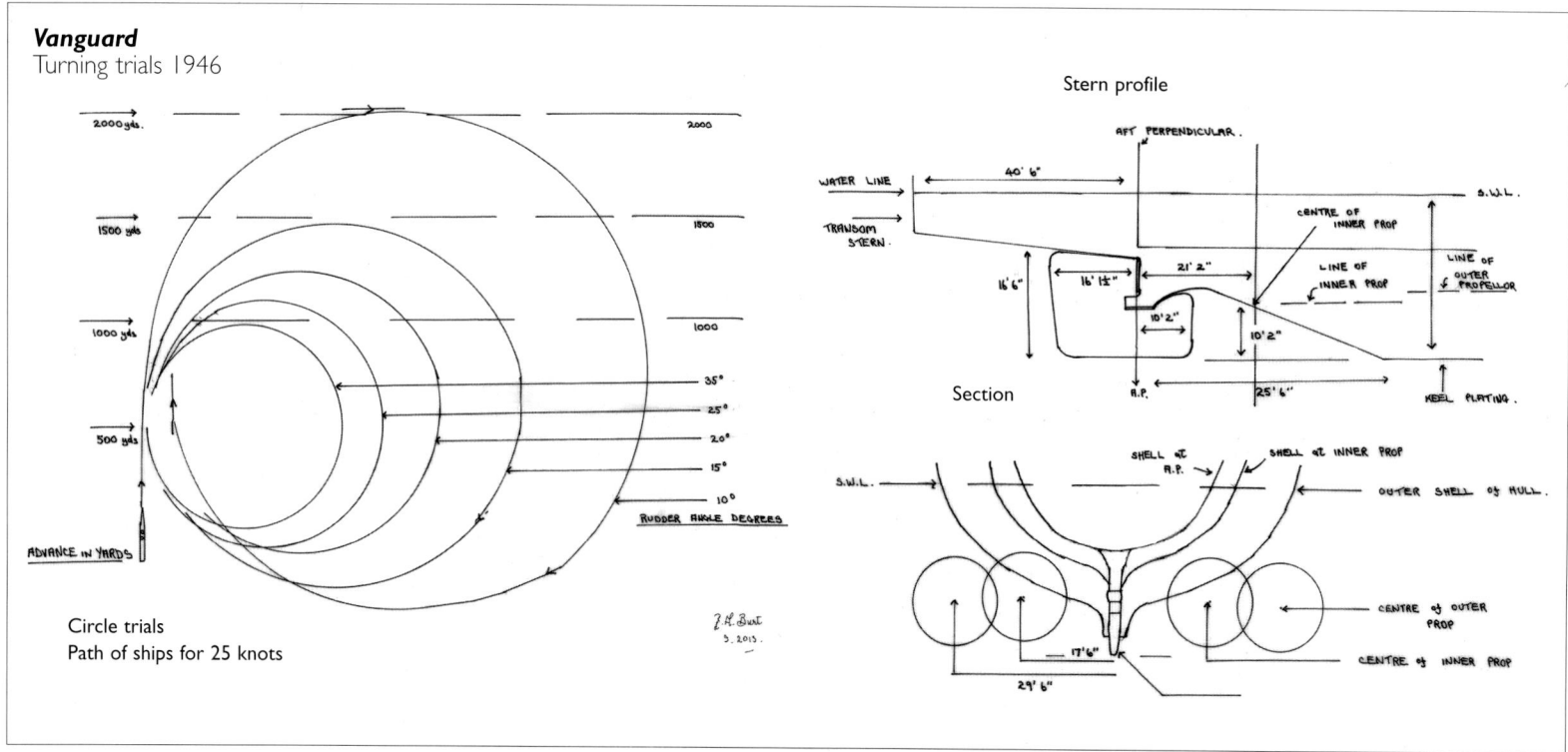

Vanguard Turning trials 1946

Circle trials
Path of ships for 25 knots

Stern profile

Section

Right: After her first gunnery trials off the coast of Ireland the *Vanguard* enters Gladstone Dock, Liverpool on 23 May 1946. Note how the constant and rigorous trials have worn the paint off her plating. *Vanguard* left the dock on 15 June 1946.

Left: *Vanguard* in December 1946, showing that the twin STAAG has been removed from the top of 'B' 15in gun turret. She has received a general tidy-up and a fresh coat of paint since her trials. *Vanguard* left Portsmouth for Gibraltar on 4 December and returned to Portsmouth on 20 December 1946 whereupon she received further minor internal alterations and decoration for the Royal Tour.

Right: Vanguard amidships during her extensive sea trials. She is seen here just outside Portsmouth Harbour in the Spithead Roads. August 1946.

Below: Seen here in August 1946 after extensive steam and manoeuvring trials.

Continued from page 56

Friday 21 June	Steering, vibration and astern trials.
Saturday 22 June	Steering and vibration trials.
	4 runs at 6,000shp.
	4 runs at 12,000shp.
	6 hours at 22,400shp.
	6 hours at 30,100shp.
Monday 24 June	6 hours at 36,400shp.
	6 hours at 63,400shp.
Tuesday 25 June	Steam trial with only 2 boilers and 2 turbines in use.
Wednesday 26 June	12 hours at 73,600shp.
	12 hours at 102,000shp.
Friday 28 June	4 runs at 120,000shp.
	3 hours at 130,000shp.

From 28 June through to 11 July exhaustive trials carried out including half power, astern, circle, rudder and instrument trials before the ship left the area and proceeded to Devonport for docking.

Bridgework and Funnels

The completed bridgework seen in *Vanguard* was a far cry from many of the early designs put forward by the Test Laboratory when working on the new structure, which had been discussed for over two years. At the National Physical Laboratory models were made to see how funnel and bridge arrangements could be improved over previous classes of battleship. A model was made to a scale of ⅛in to 1ft which was mounted on a representative sea whereupon steam was projected from funnels by suitable blowers.

As shown in the drawings, the early 1943 model of the bridge was very similar to that of the *King George V* class, with twin rangefinders for the secondary guns behind the rangefinder for the main guns. Outboard the bridge face showed two sections and was on two levels. This early structure, however, did not prove successful after wind and smoke tests proved that any bridge face with sharp or steep receding sides was unsatisfactory. There were also problems with not just the shape but with the development of work to the upper part of the bridge regarding its form, draught protection and effects of air flow over the compass platform. These tests also included exploration of air flow over the upper bridge shapes, regarding the fitting of a roof or leaving it completely open to the elements.

By November 1944 tests were still underway and another model was made to improve the design structure which had been accepted. Adjustable windows were placed in different areas as well as baffles on the face and sides of the bridge. Internal floor levels were slightly altered in some cases.

Regarding baffles on the sides and face which had been a feature of earlier battleship bridges, the addition of such fittings in *Vanguard* did not show any real advantages for wind deflection and were accordingly dropped. The results of these extensive tests saw the arrangements of the modified bridge accepted and incorporated into the final design. The result was a combination of features from the *King George V*s and *Warspite/Queen Elizabeth* (as reconstructed) and as completed, *Vanguard*'s smooth, large, flat bridge face, uncluttered by platforms or sponsons, was seen as one of the best bridge designs ever fitted to a Royal Navy capital ship.

The funnels were large, narrow, streamlined fittings with permanent cowls unlike previous clinker/caps which had been added as an afterthought to many refitted battleships in the Royal Navy. *Vanguard*'s funnels were developed from a special set of wind tests to not only eliminate smoke over the bridge and control positions but to try and direct the smoke at a certain angle away from the ship. The earlier tests on the new bridge carried out from January to November 1944 also saw consideration as to funnel height, with the finished result being similar to those in the *King George V*s but raised 8ft higher than the original design (see drawings).

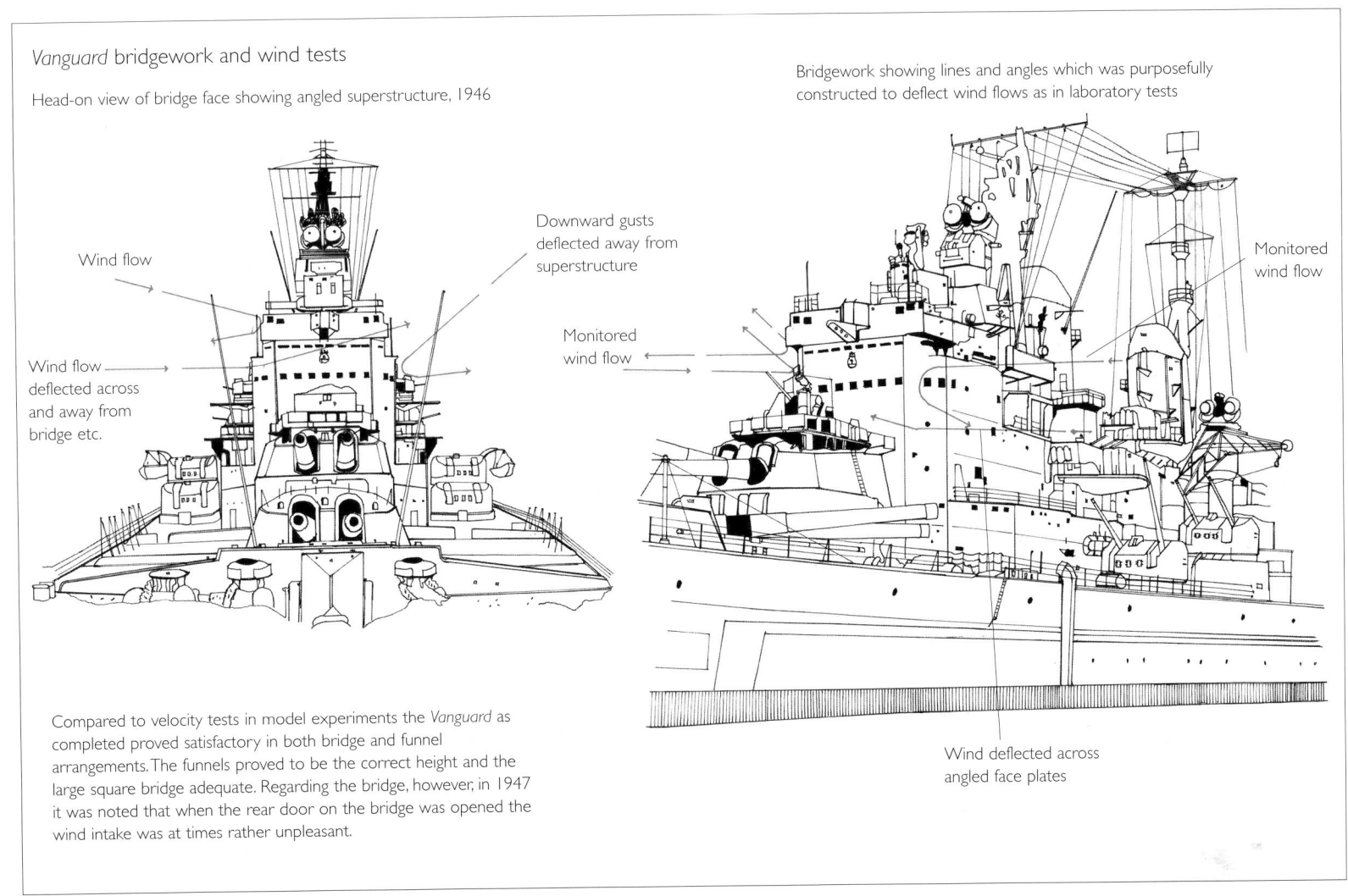

Vanguard bridgework and wind tests

Head-on view of bridge face showing angled superstructure, 1946

Bridgework showing lines and angles which was purposefully constructed to deflect wind flows as in laboratory tests

Compared to velocity tests in model experiments the *Vanguard* as completed proved satisfactory in both bridge and funnel arrangements. The funnels proved to be the correct height and the large square bridge adequate. Regarding the bridge, however, in 1947 it was noted that when the rear door on the bridge was opened the wind intake was at times rather unpleasant.

THE LAST BRITISH BATTLESHIP

Early bridge experiments for new battleship (*Vanguard*)

Vanguard's bridge and superstructure as in 1943 design.

Bridge design similar to *Lion* and *King George V* classes for *Vanguard* during tests for suitable superstructure arrangements in 1943.

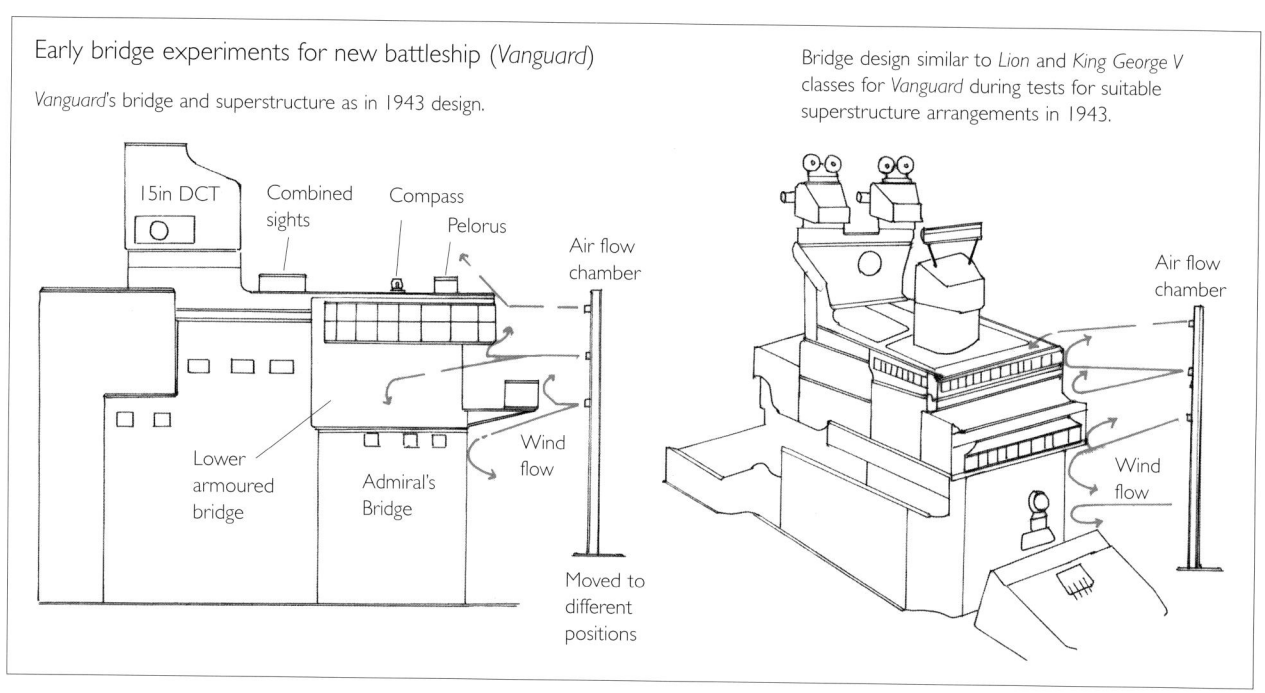

- 15in DCT
- Combined sights
- Compass
- Pelorus
- Air flow chamber
- Lower armoured bridge
- Admiral's Bridge
- Wind flow
- Moved to different positions
- Air flow chamber
- Wind flow

Vanguard wind tests for funnel height, 1946

The experiment was carried out using a wind velocity of 1–3+6, the results showing that at all forces of wind the increase in height of the funnels proved superior in keeping smoke and fumes from the bridge spaces.

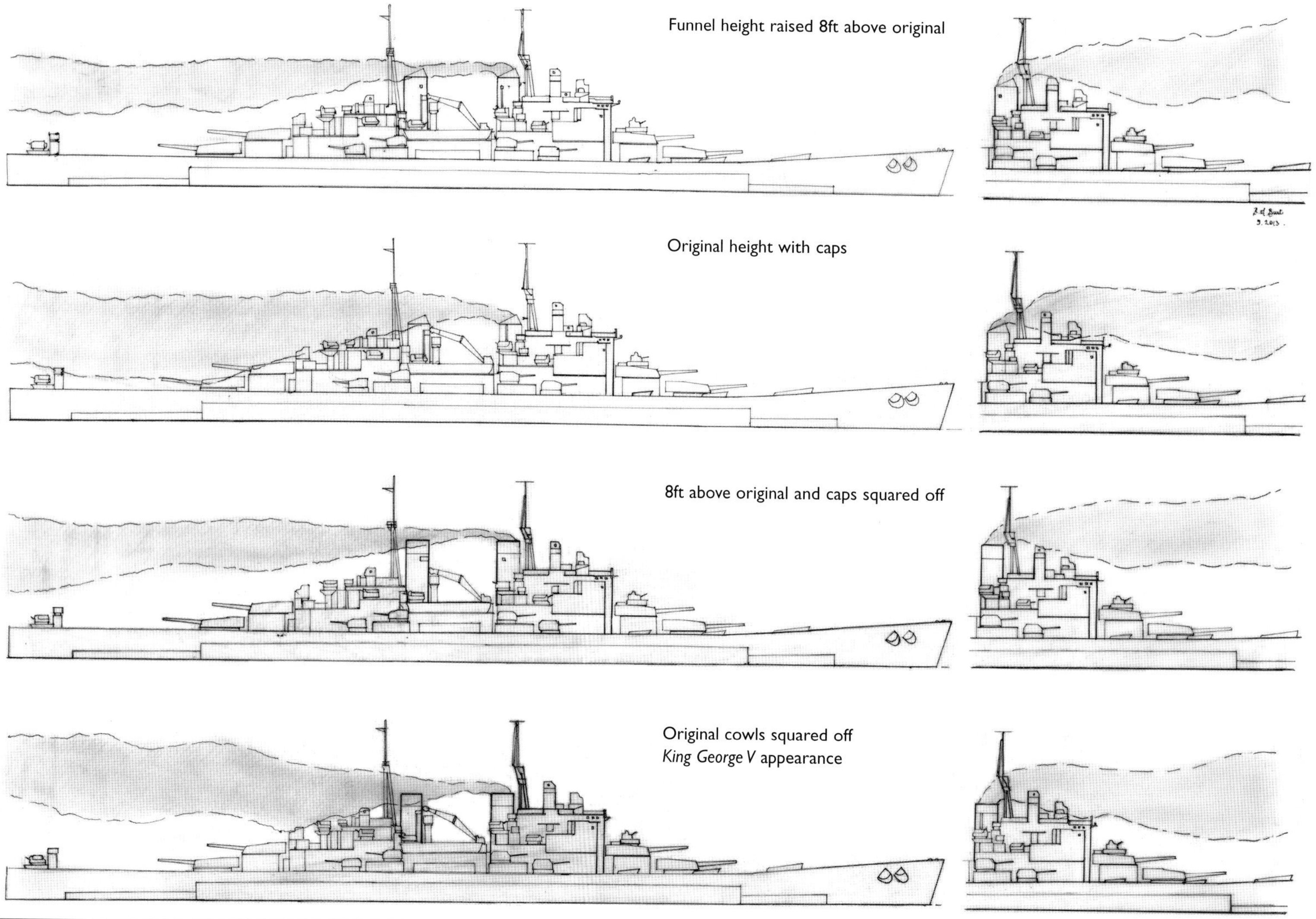

Funnel height raised 8ft above original

Original height with caps

8ft above original and caps squared off

Original cowls squared off *King George V* appearance

Above: A superb close-up of the port bow showing *Vanguard*'s remarkable flare forward. The public on board the little ships for a 'See the Fleet' trip pass by the vessel which is the star of the August 1959 Navy Day.

Right: Stern view showing *Vanguard*'s transom stern. She has been given a lick of paint for her appearance at Navy Day by the looks of it.

THE LAST BRITISH BATTLESHIP

Looking back from the forecastle over the massive bridge and forward 15in guns of *Vanguard* during Navy Day in August 1959. Already stripped of her 40mm Bofors guns (note the empty platforms on each side of the bridge), her decks are packed solid with the general public who want to take a final look at the last British battleship in existence before she is finally towed away to the scrapyard.

Ever since 1920 it had been suggested that a British Dreadnought should be preserved when Admiral Beatty's HMS *Lion* was put forward for possible preservation. Then it was Admiral Jellicoe's *Iron Duke* in the frame. Many followed, with much fuss over HMS *Warspite* in 1947 and then perhaps *Rodney* or *King George V* (which had famously sunk the *Bismarck*) *Vanguard* of course went through a very long debate over possible preservation as a museum ship, but it seems although the thought was there and highly commendable, the reality of preserving such a giant ship which was already costing over £500,000 per year whist sitting idle in Portsmouth Dockyard was simply out of the question in 1958–60. Historians reflecting on the theme of saving at least one British battleship are well aware of the enormous difficulties that would have faced such a project but in conclusion it has to be said that it is a terrible shame that with all the magnificent history of these superb vessels, that somehow, just one ship of the type regardless of cost, was not preserved for future generations to see.

Starboard broadside as she sits off Portsmouth during the summer of 1959 where she had been a familiar sight since 1956.

THE LAST BRITISH BATTLESHIP

Left: Navy Day August 1959. This photo shows her fine lines and huge bridge structure. Note that the whip aerials on bridge and fore funnel are still in place but many of the smaller radar aerials on aft funnel had been long removed.

Below: Port view of *Vanguard* as she drifts toward the shore jetty during her tow out of Portsmouth Dockyard on 4 August 1960. Note that the anchor has just been dropped to try and stop her progress.

THE LAST BRITISH BATTLESHIP

Right: *Vanguard* finally arrives at Faslane watched by dozens of locals who want a look at a British battleship that is moving for the last time.

Below: The beginning of the end as the scrapping process gets underway in the Faslane shipbreakers yard in October 1960.

Radar Equipment

Being designed and constructed during the war years, *Vanguard* naturally benefited from receiving the latest technology. By the time of her fitting-out during late 1945 and early 1946, one of the most important aspects of any warship was her radar installation and it was intended for *Vanguard* to have the best. As completed in May 1946, as far as radar was concerned she was one of the best-equipped battleships of her day.

It was obvious that the latest equipment needed to be fitted in the shortest possible time but as *Vanguard* went to sea for her trials during mid-1946 a report was produced which caused great concern as to whether or not she had been given the best radar that was available at that time.

Most of the equipment was the result of hasty wartime production which after the war was considered to have been designed too rapidly. In order to get the equipment into service quickly the first versions were simply installed aboard ships without any trials of prototypes. It was thought at the time that in many cases, and certainly for *Vanguard*, radar installations could have been improved with more peacetime tests to enhance wartime equipment.

As early as April 1946 it was proposed to employ *Vanguard* for a Royal Tour in February 1947 which meant that major trials for her radar would have to be postponed. A suggestion put forward later, however, to carry out radar tests whilst the ship was undergoing her steam trials in June 1946, and this was accepted. It was agreed by the Admiralty Signal Establishment (ASE) that as many of its personnel as possible should spend a short period on the ship. Thirty-five scientific and technical officers consisting of members of the Radar and Communication Experimental Departments and the Design and Development Divisions were to end up spending 143 days on the ship. Stringent tests were carried out on equipment under seagoing conditions and observations were also noted on vibration and interference from one radar to another, funnel gas tests and the strength of structural fittings.

As already mentioned, the *Vanguard* contained the very latest radar equipment and her size and huge complement favoured a high standard of technical performance under seagoing and wartime conditions. Even so, many of the Technical staff that visited the ship during the trials were surprised at the toll seagoing conditions took on delicate equipment.

The radar as fitted in *Vanguard* was as follows:

Type 960 Aircraft warning.
Type 293 Target indicator set.
Type 277 Warning of surface craft and height finding.
Type 268 Warning of surface craft.
Type 274 2 sets for main 15in armament.
Type 930 Fall of shot associated with Type 274.

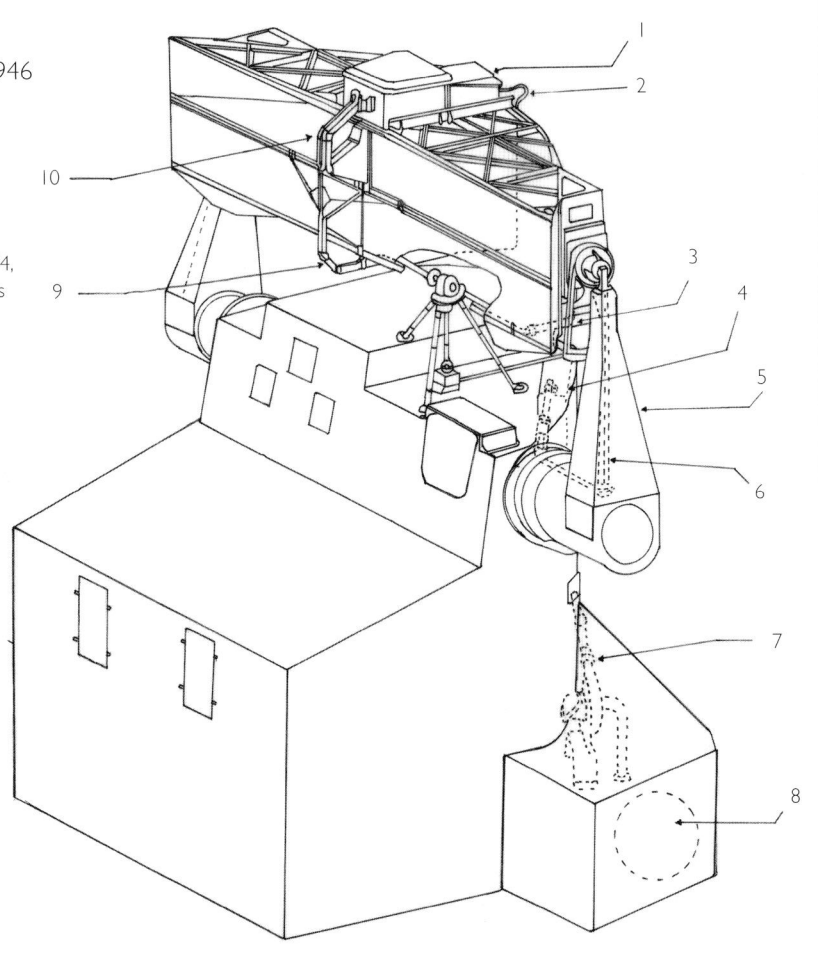

Vanguard
Director control tower showing radar equipment Type 274 stabilised array, 1946

Type 274 radar formed an integral part of the fire control arrangements for the main armament. It fed a continuous and accurate range directly into the AFCT Mk 10. Accurate target bearings could be obtained from Type 274, which could be followed continuously regardless of movement in any direction.

1. Aerial switch unit
2. Pipe from receiver to wave guide
3. Elevating arc
4. Transmitter
5. Reflector trunnion support
6. Wave guide
7. Blower (enclosed and not on show)
8. Position for long base rangefinder (removed during 1952 refit)
9. Wave guide flare
10. Guide flare

Type 275 4 sets Mk 37 for 5.25in secondary armament.
Type 262 6 sets associated with CRBF director and 1 set for the STAAG mounting on 'B' turret.

W/T Transmitters
2 x TBS 86M.
86DM.
57DMR.

W/T Receivers
21 x B28.
3 x B29.

Navigational Aids
D/F.
FM2.
RU4.

Vanguard,
Radar equipment, 1948

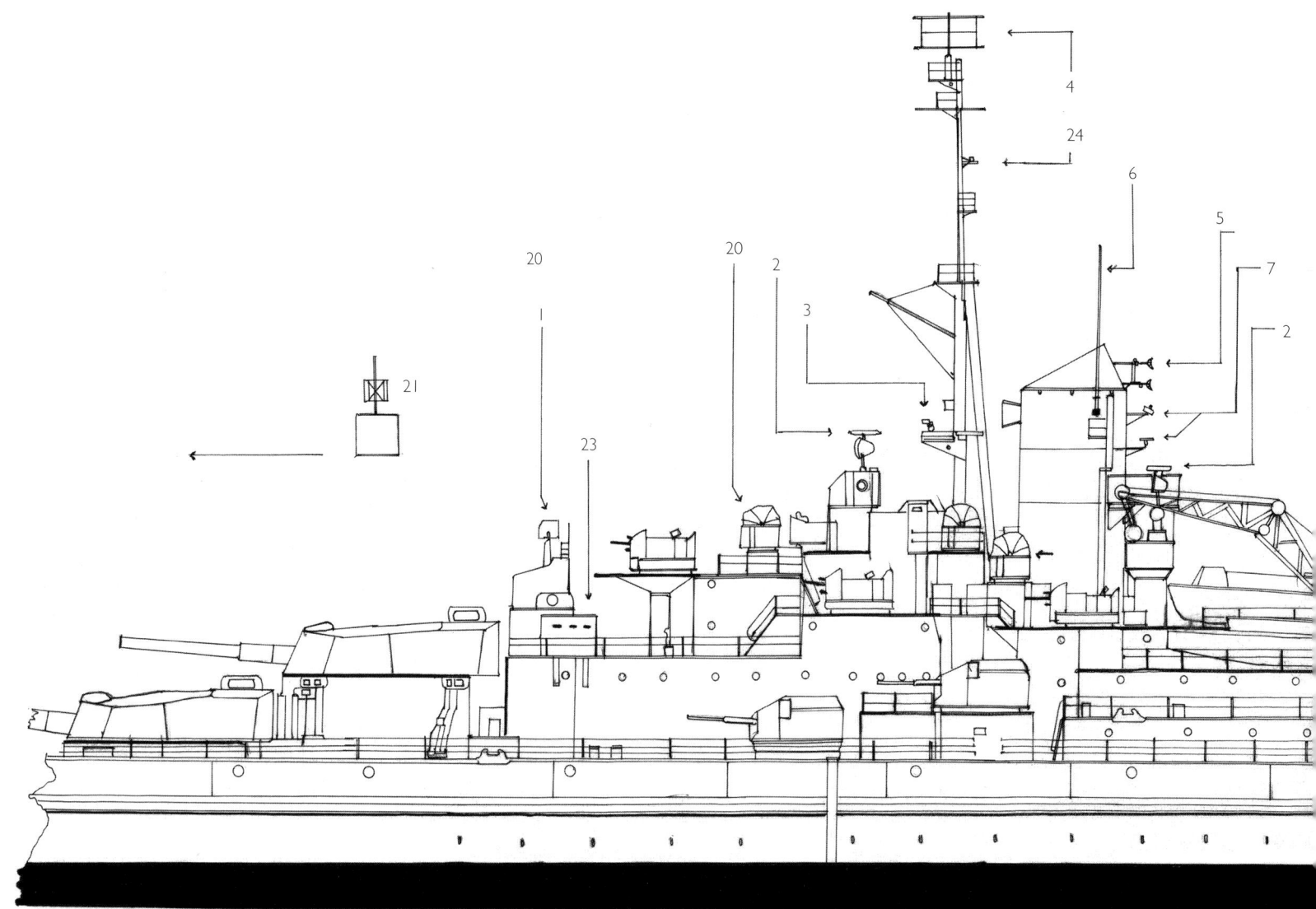

1. Type 274 for main gunnery. Double cheese type aerial. Improved version of Type 284.
2. Type 275 for 5.25in gunnery. Very large concave reflectors (twin).
3. Type 268 surface warning. Small cheese aerial with blunt ends.
4. Type 281B air warning. Rectangular framed aerial. Improved version of Type 279. Replaced later with Type 960. (Similar aerial.)
5. Type 91 TBS.
6. 30ft TBS whip aerial.
7. CXFR – US type for LAA.
8. 30ft TBS whip aerial. (2 more fitted on forecastle later.)
9. Type 293 general warning. Large double cheese aerial with pointed ends.
10. Type 86 TBS aerials.
11. Type 86 and 87M interrogator IFF (friend or foe).
12. Type 253 air interrogator IFF aerials. (same aerials for 242 IFF.)
13. Type 277 surface warning. Parabolic screen aerial.
14. Type 930 navigational set.
15. W/T office.

RADAR EQUIPMENT

IFF Interrogator sets all associated with Types 960, 277, 293 and 275.

These were other small IFF and TBS fittings which were coupled with various sets to enhance their signal.

Vanguard was also equipped with a large radar display room, operations room, auto radar plot room, aircraft defence direction and a target indicator room. These positions were all connected to the Admiral's bridge, the Captain's area and the bridge plotting offices.

The tests that were carried out in June and July alongside the steam trials, although viewed by technical staff as inadequate but necessary, were to show that many of the radar sets and associated equipment needed attention to make them work to their full potential.

Some of the main problems are highlighted here:

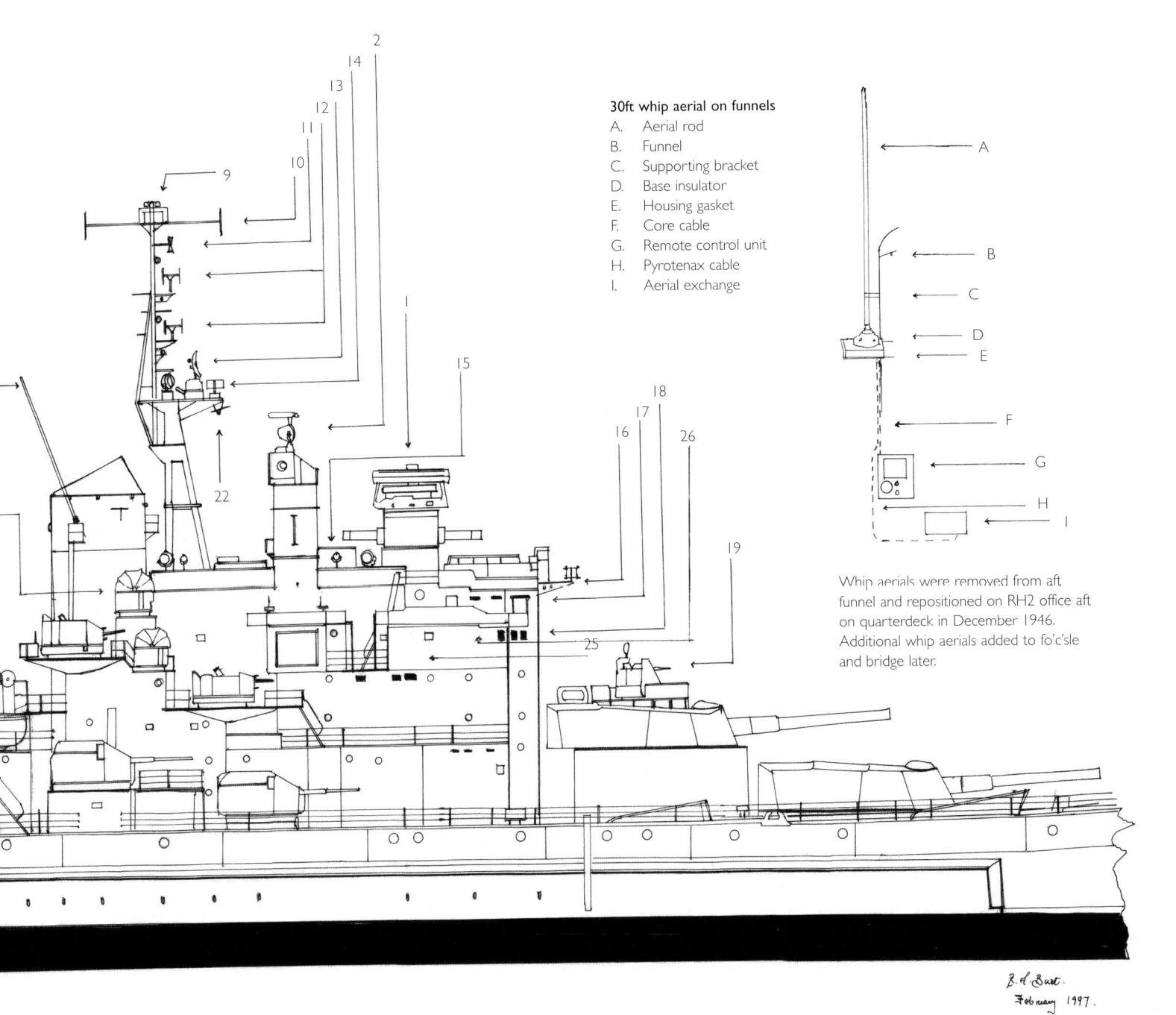

30ft whip aerial on funnels
A. Aerial rod
B. Funnel
C. Supporting bracket
D. Base insulator
E. Housing gasket
F. Core cable
G. Remote control unit
H. Pyrotenax cable
I. Aerial exchange

Whip aerials were removed from aft funnel and repositioned on RH2 office aft on quarterdeck in December 1946. Additional whip aerials added to fo'c'sle and bridge later.

16. Type FM7 M/F directional finder. Usually on face of bridge.
17. Conning tower platform.
18. Admiral's bridge.
19. STAAG 40mm mounting with Type 262 in large cupolas.
20. CRBF (close range blind fire directors). For six-barrel 40mm Bofors with 262 radar.
21. VHF directional finder fitted on quarterdeck (RH2 and office).
22. QM5 navigational set.
23. After conning position.
24. 86M and 253P.
25. Bridge receiving room and cipher office.
26. Bridge plotting room.

Separate offices for Types 293, 953, 960 main radar display, transmitting office and RCM office.
11 Metadyne rooms spread throughout ship.

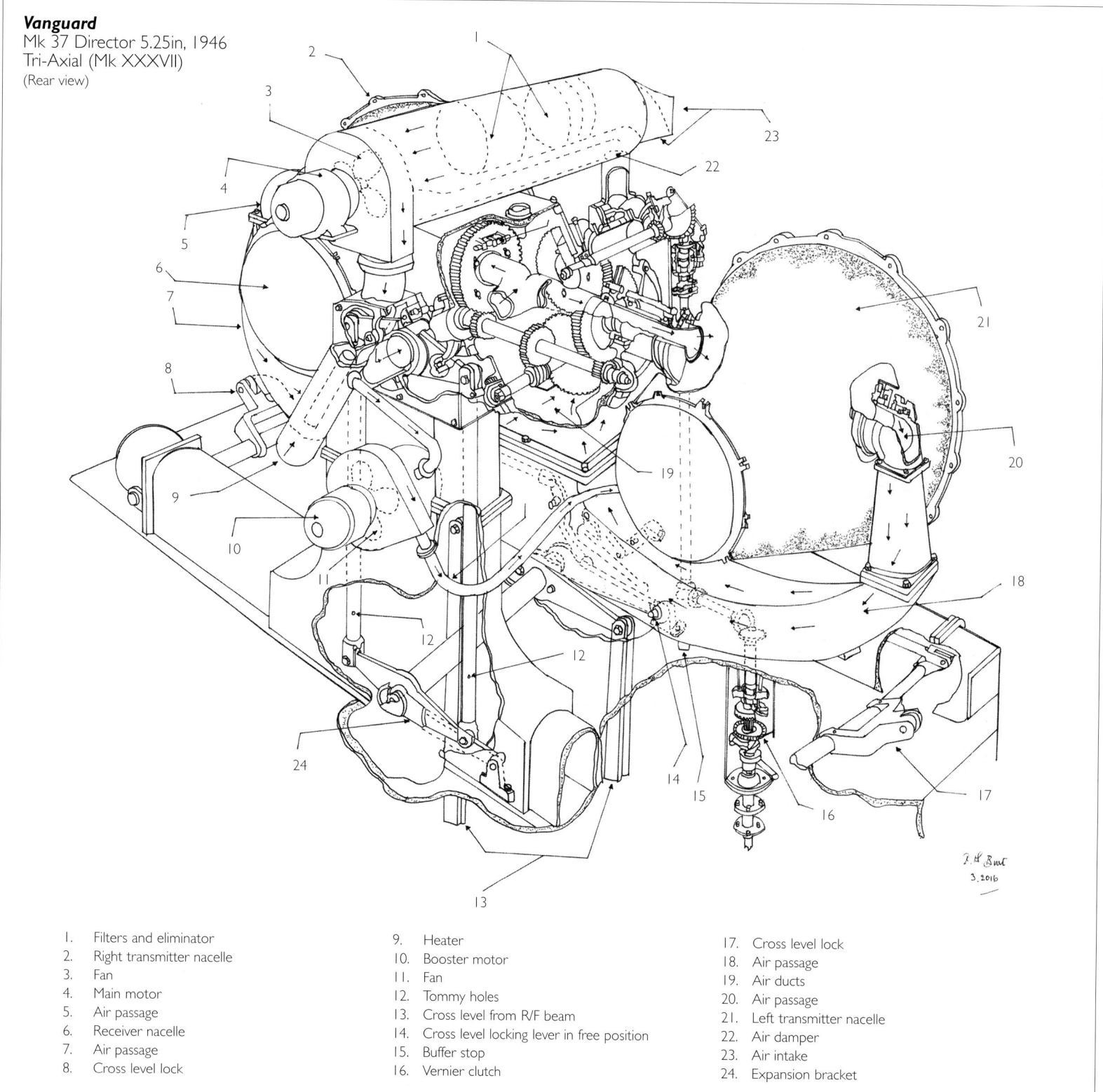

Vanguard
Mk 37 Director 5.25in, 1946
Tri-Axial (Mk XXXVII)
(Rear view)

1. Filters and eliminator
2. Right transmitter nacelle
3. Fan
4. Main motor
5. Air passage
6. Receiver nacelle
7. Air passage
8. Cross level lock
9. Heater
10. Booster motor
11. Fan
12. Tommy holes
13. Cross level from R/F beam
14. Cross level locking lever in free position
15. Buffer stop
16. Vernier clutch
17. Cross level lock
18. Air passage
19. Air ducts
20. Air passage
21. Left transmitter nacelle
22. Air damper
23. Air intake
24. Expansion bracket

- Type 274. Although the set was viewed as the most accurate and up-to-date fire control system for a ships main armament in existence at that time which was also coupled to a superb Admiralty Fire Control Table which gave the range and bearing plots, the tests showed there was terrible trouble with the commutator and other connections.
- Type 960. It proved difficult to line up the bearing indicator of this set when the ship yawed or changed direction. When all other sets were working the Type 960 display proved to be of little operational use and needed adjustment.
- Type 275. The mountings needed improvement and vibration was a serious problem.
- Type 262. Transmission faults showed themselves and there was overheating of certain small fittings within the system. Also the Type 262 CRBF on the quarterdeck was unsuitable given the vibration in that area.

Some aerials also showed interference with other sets and radar rooms were seen to be stuffy and needed more ventilation. Each set was constantly switched on and off to see just what sets interfered

RADAR EQUIPMENT

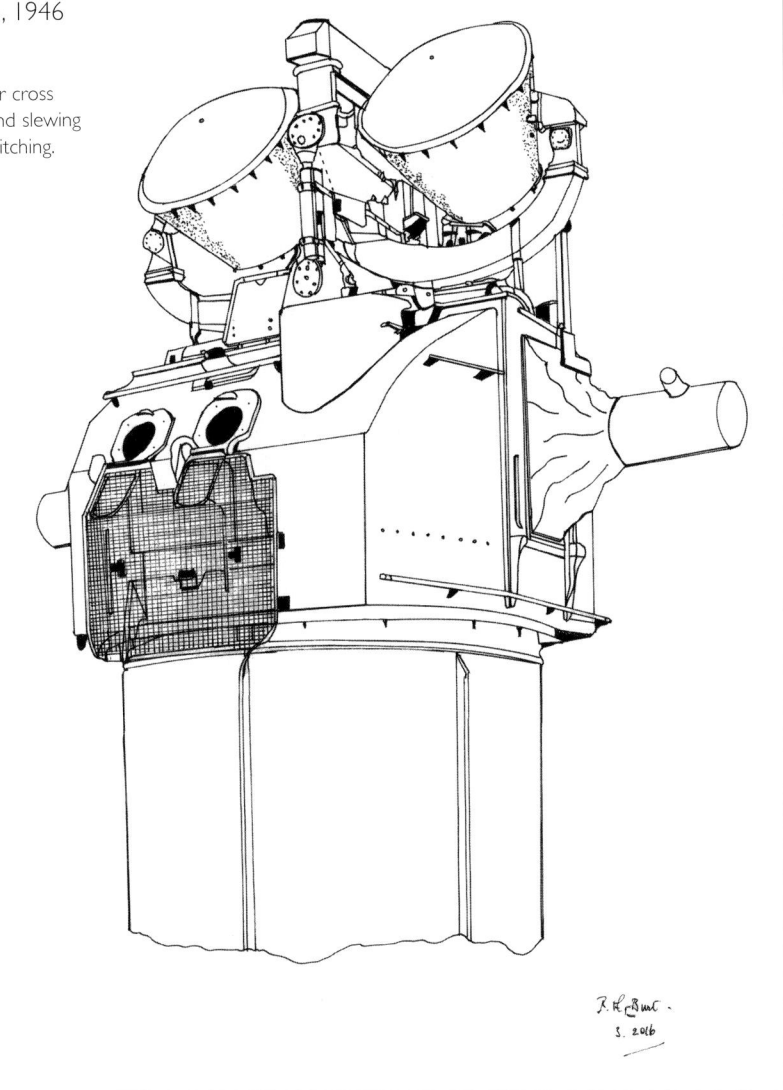

Vanguard Mk 37 Director (5.25in control), 1946 (front view)

The Mk 37 Director was a tri-axial director. Drives for cross level were taken to the rangefinder, the radar array and slewing sight horizontal even when the ship was rolling and pitching.

Crew to operate system were:
1. Director — Layer, trainer and range taker.
2. Computer — No 1 and one hand.
3. Radar — Layer, trainer, and range taker.
4. Guns — Captain, layer and trainer.

with others. Transmission, auto-aligning, safety and power supplies all came under the most rigorous examination by the ASE staff.

This visit to *Vanguard* proved to be a success and provided the opportunity to observe the very latest in radar technology and also show how important it was to get technical staff together with Admiralty personnel and to liaise with one another.

The final conclusion was that however excellent individual radar sets may be, both in their conception and performance, an insufficient amount of thought had gone into providing the ship with a unified and harmonious radar plan.

Of course these minor problems were not just confined to the Royal Navy but were to appear on all foreign warships as staff tried to cope with the ever-increasing pace of technological development. There is no doubt that we still have many teething problems today.

Type 274 Radar

The Type 274 radar provided a radar range set which formed an integral part of the fire control for the 15in guns. The set fed a continuous and accurate range directly into the Admiralty Fire Control Table (AFCT) Mk 10. This was matched up with other fire-control tables. The range was then determined by a range rate transmission unit fitted to the face of the range display panel. Accurate target bearing was obtained from the Type 274 and changes in the bearing were followed.

Considerable attention had been paid to the fall of the shot and a special spotting display was fitted. *Vanguard* had two Type 274 sets, above each of the main 15in gun directors fore and aft.

Also, arrangements were made in *Vanguard* for her Type 277 set to be able to switch to ranging and spotting in the event of a breakdown in the Type 274 aerial on either DCT.

The ranges for the Type 274 were:

1. Battleship to battleship   42,000 yds
2. Battleship to cruiser   40,000 yds
3. Battleship to destroyer   38,000 yds

The Type 274 set had a range discrimination of 100 yards and an excellent bearing ability. At the time of installation it was considered to be one of the finest pieces of equipment for main gun fire control.

The Royal Tour of 1947

Below: HM King George VI's sleeping cabin for the Royal Tour. The King and Queen also had a day cabin each. For the King's cabin the Queen chose a chair covering with galleons in full sail on a sea green background with knotted ropes. Cushions were coral and sepia, the furniture was all mahogany and lighting was provided from shell wall brackets painted ivory and sepia. The carpet was mushroom and beige. The Queen's day cabin was fitted with maize-coloured curtains, satinwood furniture and similar carpet to the King's and covers for the settee and chairs to match the curtains while the rest of the furniture had coverings of celadon ground cretonne with a floral design of apricot and ivory.

It became public knowledge in April/May 1946 that the new battleship *Vanguard* was to take HM King George VI, the Queen, Princess Elizabeth and Princess Margaret on a trip to South Africa. The Royal Family had been invited by the South African Prime Minister Field Marshal Smuts and the gratefully-accepted invitation was seen as a goodwill visit to enhance the relationship between the two countries after the Second World War and also a chance to show the flag in the Royal Navy's latest capital ship.

To accommodate the Royal Party *Vanguard* underwent many modifications in the aft superstructure. The cabins of the Admiral, Captain of the Fleet and the Chief of Staff, as well as the Staff Office, were modified and re-arranged for the Royal Family. No new provision was made for the officers who had been displaced by the move. The accommodation for the Royal staff, ladies in waiting, maids, stewards etc, was all arranged in existing spaces and compartments were slightly altered as necessary.

The radar aerial was removed from the mainmast to accommodate a tall flagpole for the Royal Standard and the 40mm STAAG mount was removed from the roof of 'B' 15in gun turret and replaced with a viewing platform with a small protective surround fitted to it. There was also a canopy that could be placed over it for shade etc, when necessary. Further small modifications saw the removal of some of the 40mm Bofors guns. There was also additional advanced radio and long-distance communication equipment installed in different parts of the ship and special radio-telephony receiver equipment fitted in the Royal quarters.

The Royal Party travelled down to Portsmouth Dockyard on 31 January 1947 and boarded *Vanguard* at 16.35 hours.

Their Majesties with their Royal Highnesses The Princess Elizabeth and The Princess Margaret embarked in *Vanguard* at

Left: Two views showing the sleeping cabin of Princess Elizabeth.

Left: On 1 February 1947 *Vanguard* sails between the vessels of the Home Fleet at a speed of 10 knots. All ships were dressed with masthead flags and the crews were massed along the decks. As the *Vanguard* approached the battleships and cruisers a 21-gun salute was fired as she came abreast each ship with the crews giving three loud cheers for the Royal Family. During the manoeuvre the Royal Family stood on the special platform on 'B' turret with the King saluting each ship as they passed by. The King gave the order to 'Splice the Mainbrace' on all ships participating in the event as a thank-you to the ships in the Home Fleet.

Right: *Vanguard* arrived at Cape Town in South Africa on 17 February 1947, a beautiful clear sunny day, and berthed alongside Duncan Dock as seen in the photograph. The King inspected a Royal Marine Guard of Honour before leaving the ship to be greeted with a fantastic reception from the people waiting to see the Royal Family. They were met by Field Marshal Smuts and other dignitaries before slowly driving off to Government House. The Royal Party stayed in Cape Town for three days before setting off for their tour of South Africa.

Below: HM Queen Elizabeth's sleeping cabin. The photo shows Corporal Rogers of the Royal Marines who was appointed Batman to the King and Queen for the journey. All photos were taken between 27 and 29 January 1947.

THE ROYAL TOUR OF 1947

Left: Whilst in dock the ship was, at certain times, open to the public and children's parties were held on board. After this there were some tactical exercises carried out in local waters before visiting other ports (see Royal Tour notes). A stern view of *Vanguard* still fully dressed with plenty of locals still eager to see her. Note the special platform covered in red carpet on the right which was built for the Royal Family when they first left the ship.

Below: *Vanguard* alongside at Durban. She berthed there on 11 April and stayed for six days.

South Railway Jetty, Portsmouth at 16.35 on 31st January 1947. Her Majesty Queen Mary the Right Honourable the Duke of Gloucester, the Princess Royal and her Royal Highness the Duchess of Kent came on board with them to say goodbye. Fortunately the weather had cleared soon after the noon and it was fine and cold after a week of snow and frost. The rest of the Royal Family left the ship at 17.50.

The *Vanguard* slipped her moorings from the Railway Jetty at 07.20 hours in poor visibility owing to the fact that Great Britain was experiencing one of the worst winters on record and the snow and mist had returned. The weather was so cold that two nights before the Royal Party arrived one of the glass shields on the captain's bridge shattered owing to the frost. Nevertheless, two days later the ship moved off to the music of the massed bands and cheers from the public.

At 10.40 hours on 1 February *Vanguard* set sail and passed through two columns of the Home Fleet. HMS *Implacable*, *Cleopatra*, *Diadem* and *St James* broke away from the line to join *Vanguard* as an escort. Three helicopters flew overhead with one landing on the quarterdeck of *Vanguard* to pick up press photographs and other related material.

At 15.00 hours the French battleship *Richelieu* and two destroyers made an appearance one mile off *Vanguard*'s starboard beam and fired a Royal salute. The weather was still foul, however, with a wind force of 7–8 and heavy rain.

On 7 February, eight miles off Cape Verde lighthouse, *Vanguard* stopped and launched her barge to take the Royal Family across to the aircraft carrier *Implacable* for a visit during which they inspected the crew and watched displays etc.

Vanguard finally arrived at Cape Town, South Africa on 17 February 1947 whereupon the Royal Family left the ship for their tour of the country

Whilst the Royal Party were away on their travels the *Vanguard* visited the ports of Durban and Simonstown and then returned to Cape Town, with the ship being open to the public. The following figures of visitors were recorded:

Cape Town: 22 February =   6,500
             23 February = 10,778

Right: Back on *Vanguard*, the Royal Family prepare to leave Cape Town and South Africa. The King and his family can be seen walking along the quarterdeck.

Left: On the return journey from South Africa the *Vanguard* was met by a cruiser escort and the aircraft carrier *Triumph* on 7 May. The Queen and the two Princesses transferred over to the carrier for a visit. The King did not accompany them owing to him not being well. Princess Margaret is seen shaking hands with the Captain.

THE ROYAL TOUR OF 1947

Left: The Queen and the two Princesses on deck of HMS *Triumph* whilst being shown around the ship and about to inspect some of the crew.

Below: The crew of HMS *Triumph* line the deck to wave and cheer the Royal Family and *Vanguard* as she continues her homeward voyage. As a thank-you for the hospitality from *Triumph*, the crew line the decks of *Vanguard* to cheer and bid them farewell.

Having just completed her 11,000-mile return voyage from South Africa, *Vanguard* finally enters home waters. Shown here on her way to moor alongside the South Railway Jetty, she passes the old Portsea wall watched by thousands of well-wishers all waving and cheering the Royal Family who can be seen standing on the platform atop 'B' turret.

Simonstown:	8 March	=	1,194
Durban:	2 April	=	6,600
	3 April	=	8,900
	6 April	=	11,000
Cape Town:	12 April	=	2,539
	13 April	=	1,750
Total:			**49,761**

These figures do not include the many visits by special guests or Government officials.

After a very successful tour the Royal Family returned to the ship and *Vanguard* left South Africa on 24 April, visiting St Helena and the Ascension Islands before reaching Portsmouth on 12 May where she was greeted by thousands of well-wishers spread out from Southsea to Portsmouth Dockyard.

In October 1947 a previous request to ascertain the costs of *Vanguard's* modifications for the Royal trip was forwarded to the Admiralty from Portsmouth. The costs were as follows: £169,129 of which £29,629 was for special furnishings and special items of stores.

After the Royal Tour the *Vanguard* docked at Portsmouth and remained there until June, finally leaving for Devonport and a minor refit. In March 1948 it was announced that she would undertake another Royal Tour in early 1949. Because of this news the impending trials that had been planned for *Vanguard* would either have to be postponed or restricted, especially those for gunnery due to possible damage to delicate equipment on board for the Royal Family. A letter from the Director of Training and Staff Duties (DTSD) to Admiralty staff laid down the requirements:

It is now unlikely that the programme of trials outlined can be carried out in full before *Vanguard* sails for the next Royal Tour on or about 15th February 1949. It may, however, be possible to progress certain of the trials depending on the date the ship is taken in hand for re-alteration, the date of commissioning to

Before disembarking the Royal Family say their goodbyes to the crew. The Queen, Princess Elizabeth and Princess Margaret are seen here waiting for the King.

Moored alongside the South Railway Jetty the Royal Family leave *Vanguard*. The King leads the Queen and the two Princesses back onto British soil. *Vanguard* is fully dressed and manned, as well as the railway platform being crammed full with officials, Press photographers, military personnel and brass bands etc.

full complement, final painting and preparation, and certain other factors. It is also probable that full or partial restrictions will be placed on the firing of the main armament. The DTSD has been directed to look into the possibility of arranging a reduced programme of trials.

Two alternatives were suggested:

1. Main armament firing completely prohibited.
2. One-gun salvoes from 'A' turret allowed.

It would seem that the first suggestion would strongly hamper the navy's ongoing trials, but by using 'A' 15in turret only this would not disturb paintwork or fittings aft of the ship where the Royal Family had their quarters, and in most cases spent all of their leisure time on the quarterdeck rarely venturing near the forward 15in guns, foc's'le and anchor equipment. Therefore it was accepted that limited one-gun salvoes be permitted for trial purposes.

The correspondence continued:

> The decision has been taken because damage to any of the special equipment or the special preparation of the superstructure for the final coat of enamel or paint (none of which is designed to withstand the blast or shock of gunfire) is unacceptable, since much damage would materially increase the amount of dockyard work involved after the cruise.

The trial requirements were quite extensive, including the following:

  5.25in RPC trials.
  5.25in trials with Mk VII fuse-setting machine in conjunction with computer system.
  Sea trials for the six-barrel Bofors 40mm mounts.
  15in RPC trials.
  Mk 274 Auto follow trials.
  Mk X AFCT trials.
  Type 931 radar trials.
  Communication trials involving Type 603, 57DMR aerial.
  Roll, yaw and pitch trials.

With this in mind the *Vanguard* left Devonport for Gibraltar in September 1948 and carried out trials in order of importance on various equipment and fittings where possible, taking into consideration the above restrictions. The Royal Tour in the spring of 1949 was to take the King, Queen and Princess Margaret to New Zealand and Australia. In November 1948, however, the trip was suddenly cancelled due to the King's failing health.

A further Royal Tour was put forward for March 1952 which would see the Royal Family going back to the Cape for a rather long visit to help the King who was recovering from a serious lung operation. Sadly this never happened owing to the fact that the King died in his sleep on 6 February 1952.

Appearance Changes

From an appearance point of view the *Vanguard* was unique in many ways. Her principal characteristics were as follows:

1. Flush deck with extremely steep upward sheer right forward and a deep bow flare.
2. Straight cutaway stem and flat square-cut stern, the latter being completely unique in a British battleship
3. Simple large square-cut bridge tower without the complexity of platforms or projections as in the *King George V*s.
4. Tall, thin streamlined funnels with small distinctive caps, turned backwards.
5. Masts and funnels closely grouped amidships.

Her rig was light for a battleship, with tripod masts that had forward-raking legs, no control top and a striking topmast to the foremast which was stepped abaft. The mainmast was a single pole above the tripod with radar aerials at the head of each topmast. For the first time there were also whip antennae, on the forecastle, at the sides of the bridge, on each funnel and aft next to the 40mm AA mount.

Although it could be said that in general she was less piled-up than the *King George V*s, she was more cluttered amidships and on the aft superstructure. This, together with her many small radar aerials and communication beacons as well as small fittings on both funnels, gave her a much heavier appearance than in previous classes.

Many did not like *Vanguard*'s appearance, suggesting that she had a slight foreign look, but she did in fact look very much like a modified and slightly longer *King George V*. It was the funnel caps which gave her her unusual and distinctive appearance.

As completed and right up to the end of her career her appearance was virtually unchanged and it is extremely difficult to date photographs of her. There were a few small modifications and the following notes are some of the visual aids that can be considered:

In late 1946 she was refitted for the Royal Tour:

- Single-barrel 40mm mounts each side of the superstructure and on the quarterdeck were removed.
- Twin STAAG 40mm mount on 'B' 15in turret was replaced grandstand platform with a removable roof.
- Single 40mm mounts on after superstructure and on quarterdeck near 'Y' turret were removed.
- There were alterations within the aft quarters to accommodate the Royal Family for the tour but this did not change her appearance in any way.
- Her Type 281 radar aerial at the head of the mainmast was removed to accommodate the Royal Standard.

1951–2: The 40mm director was removed from the quarterdeck. The twin STAAG on 'B' turret had been replaced by this date as was the flagpole on mainmast (radar back in place). Extensions on the main 15in rangefinder both fore and aft were taken off.
1952–3: Type 974 navigational radar fitted to foretop.
1954–6: Some AA guns removed.
1958–9: All 40mm guns and directors removed. Partially mothballed.

Right: *Vanguard* moored alongside in Portsmouth Dockyard after the Royal Tour. She was kept here until the end of June 1947 when she then sailed down to Devonport for a refit.

Battleship Design after *Vanguard*

As the launch of *Vanguard* drew near in November 1944, the Admiralty had set up a committee to investigate the next generation of battleship construction.

With wartime experience on their side, many suggestions were put forward to try and develop a ship which would be suitable for any future conflict. There was a great deal of anxiety during the discussions as to whether or not the Royal Navy really needed new battleships given the existing battleships' performance during the present war and the fact that aircraft-carriers and their aircraft were proving to be the most effective and useful weapon against enemy warships.

There were those who believed that there should still be large well-armed battleships which would be in the front line of any engagement at sea, and those who favoured either scrapping battleships altogether, since the age of the classic big-gun engagement was over, or if fresh construction was absolutely necessary, then building larger numbers of smaller, less powerful surface combatants might well be the answer to the Royal Navy's requirements

Those who favoured smaller ships put forward a design which was designated as 'Battleship X' and then compared it with existing battleships.

On the other side of the argument was the much larger vessel with many versions put forward but naturally based on the previously cancelled *Lion* and *Temeraire* (1943) which had been fitted with a full armament of nine 16in guns.

The DTSD issued the following remarks against the design of 'Battleship X':

DESIGN 'X' COMPARED WITH EXISTING BATTLESHIPS

	Design 'X'	King George V	Vanguard	US Iowa
Standard displacement:	35,800 tons	35,000 tons	42,300 tons	45,000 tons
Speed:	29 knots	28½ knots	30 knots	32½ knots
Endurance:	6,000 miles @ 20 knots	5,000 @ 20 knots	6,000 @ 20 knots	11,800 @ 20 knots
Main armament:	6 × 16in	10 × 14in	8 × 15in	9 × 16in
Secondary armament:	16 × 4.5in	16 × 5.25in	16 × 5.25in	20 × 5in
AA armament:	54 × 40mm	72 × 40mm	60 × 40mm	76 × 40mm
Armour protection:	9in side	14–15in side	13–14in side	13½in side
	6–4in deck	5–6in deck	5–6in deck	5in deck

PARTICULARS OF THE LARGE BATTLESHIP

Displacement:	67,000–70,000 tons.
Length:	950–1,000ft.
Beam:	120ft.
Draught:	35–35ft 6in.
Speed:	26–29 knots.
Endurance:	6,000 miles @ 20 knots.
SHP:	160,000.
Armament:	9 × 16in (120rpg).
Protection:	15in sides, 6in and 4in over decks with special attention to internal longitudinal bulkheads.
Cost:	£13,250,000.

The function of a battleship as defined by the Naval Staff in the document for Staff requirements for *Lion* (February 1945) is:- The basis of the strength of the Fleet is the battleship. Besides providing support for all classes of ship the battleship is the

Below: *Vanguard* in Devonport Dockyard in autumn 1947, where she remained until the autumn of 1948.

Right: *Vanguard* was always a favourite with the press and general public and when she opened her gangway for visitors there was never a shortage of people waiting to fill her decks and get a closer look at not only the largest British battleship, but one of the only ships of her type left.

most powerful unit for destroying the enemy's surface forces once they are brought to gun action. A heavier broadside than the enemy is still a very telling weapon in a naval action. In effect this means that the battleship must be able to stand up (i.e. give and take punishment) to any other type of ship afloat. Can design X achieve this function?

The most powerful ship afloat today is probably the American battleship *Iowa* and a ship not yet designed is seen to be markedly inferior to a ship already in commission.

King George V was compared with 'Battleship X' and it was pointed out that although designed over ten years ago, she was still viewed as more than comparable with this smaller type of battleship now being investigated. The six 16in of the new design were viewed as slightly inferior to the ten 14in aboard the already-existing ships. Certainly the armour protection did not come up to requirements for modern big-gun engagements and the meagre 9in main belt could be perforated at all ranges by a 16in shell.

Those on the Committee who favoured the large, powerful battleship stated:

The size of the battleship is an absolute and not a relative question. IF we embark on building anything but the most powerful and best protected ship that is possible we are committed to a definite programme which will allow any potential enemy to build something bigger and better. If out battleships are to be instruments to make war they must be relatively more powerful than those of the enemy. If our battleships are to be instruments of peace they must be relatively more powerful than any which an enemy could have which is the same thing as saying as powerful as possible, i.e. absolute power.

Alongside these deliberations, funds were being allocated toward the development of a new, improved 16in gun which would be mounted in any new capital ships which the Admiralty might lay down. Moreover the American *Iowa* was being compared with *Vanguard* and the size of that ship was seen by many as meeting the present requirements for the size of new British construction.

The conclusion of the construction Committee was delivered shortly after the cessation of hostilities in 1945 with a strong recommendation toward larger powerful ships but against this was the general mood and financial position of Great Britain after six years of hostilities. Although studied in detail, any new battleship construction was quickly dismissed – certainly for the foreseeable future. In 1945, it was generally accepted within the Admiralty that *Vanguard* was to be the last British battleship.

Overleaf: One of *Vanguard*'s engine rooms.

Below: Superb aerial view of *Vanguard* underway on 4 September 1948.

BATTLESHIP DESIGN AFTER VANGUARD

An unusual angle looking up at the foremast, showing ladders, yards and various spars.

Left: The long bow of *Vanguard* crashes through the waves during the NATO Operation 'Mariner' in September 1953.

Right: Even though *Vanguard* was a new battleship, it did not stop the old naval traditions being maintained and the rum ration was one of the oldest and most favourite of all.

Below: *Vanguard* sailing out of Malta harbour in the spring of 1949.

Criticism of *Vanguard* and the Demise of the Battleship

Vanguard had completed in the spring of 1946, which was about the same time as the question of finding a suitable role for a battleship was very much under investigation. The subject continued to be debated and by 1949 the issue became even more serious and it was frequently asked what was a battleship's purpose if the enemy did not possess this type of vessel in their own fleet. There were no more German or Japanese battleships and the possibility of the Soviet Union building and completing such ships was doubtful.

Vanguard had completed a successful Royal Tour in early 1947 and had been through extensive trials since her completion, in fact these were still ongoing as late as 1949. A rather parsimonious government was at loggerheads with the Admiralty regarding the retention of battleships and although *Vanguard*'s demise was not mentioned at this early date there were a few in the Admiralty who agreed with the government ministers that the situation should be reviewed. In general, however, in 1949, most of the Admiralty were firm about the need to retain the five remaining battleships left in service (four *King George V*s and *Vanguard*)

Between 1947 to 1949, all the battleships constructed during the First World War had gone to the scrapyard, including those that had been extensively modernised during the 1930s (*Queen Elizabeth*, *Valiant*, *Warspite* and *Renown*). *Nelson* and *Rodney* soon followed them. These warships had been part of British naval history for over thirty years and the vessels had been extremely popular, not only with the general public but throughout the Service as well. These had been the ships to which the public flocked to on Navy Days, dockyard open days and fleet reviews and many saw them as old friends. Although the Press handled the subject with sadness and sympathy, the Admiralty were still quick to issue statements to appease an uneasy public, stating that their scrapping was not only due to a manpower shortage but the fact that these warships were old, slow and worn out and had no place in a modern post-war fleet.

Not only was this disposal of battleships highly controversial, it was also being viewed by many as marking the decline of British maritime power and it was suggested that certainly once it had started it would be extremely difficult to reverse. Moreover, it was believed by some to show signs of weakness to foreign powers.

During this period of reducing the Fleet, there was much talk of rearming certain ships with the latest missile equipment but looking across to the United States saw that they were only refitting large cruisers with this type of weapon, not battleships. The Admiralty did examine this subject but it was found to be far too expensive and rather complicated in a large ship that was not originally built for the role. What the public were not being told was that it was not only the older battleships that were being dispensed with but the remaining ships from the 1936 estimates (*King George V* class) were also under the spotlight regarding their suitability in a modern atomic war. These four ships were not only the latest in technology but also only ten years old.

Shortly after the end of the war, there had been a call to 'scrap the lot' from certain parties within Government as had been the case after the First World War when all pre-dreadnoughts and many newer battleships were placed on the disposal list. None were more outspoken against than Winston Churchill and whilst

Left: *Vanguard* opens up with 15in gun salvoes during extensive gunnery trials off Malta on 3 May 1949.

debating the subject in Parliament in 1948 stated: 'You are welcome to your slogan "scrap the lot" but for my part, I prefer when I look along Government front benches, Lord Fisher's famous dictum, "sack the lot".' The First Lord of the Admiralty, Lord Hall did not agree with Churchill, however, and he and others favoured a limited disposal plan. The debate was ongoing but Churchill delivered a rather heavy broadside in March 1948 when he said: 'I say the Government ought to be ashamed and those responsible for this mishandling of our forces ought to be punished by every suitable means known to the country.'

It proved to be a losing battle, however, and statements began to appear, with this one in June 1949 by the First Lord of the Admiralty: 'My colleagues on the Defence Committee will wish to be aware of certain proposals which I have approved regarding the future employment of the five battleships in the Royal Navy. Briefly, the intention is to organise the Training Squadron and reduce all the battleships but one, to Reserve.' The basic plan was as follows:

- *King George V* was to be released from training duties and reduced to Category C Reserve whereupon she was moth-balled and laid up in the Clyde.
- *Howe*, after a short refit, was to be placed in Category A Reserve at Devonport but would be available to relieve *Vanguard* if that ship was required for another purpose such as a Royal Tour.
- *Duke of York* was to be placed in Category C Reserve at Portsmouth.
- *Anson* was to be placed in Category C Reserve in the Forth without a refit.
- *Vanguard* was to join the Training Squadron on her return from the Mediterranean.

By placing the battleships in Reserve and leaving them in this condition for a while, the public might come to think that they were no longer required.

Service opinion put forward made its way to the press, as in the *Hampshire Telegraph* of 17 June 1949:

> The Navy is finding it difficult in manning battleships owing to the current manpower shortage but as the 1st Sea Lord (Admiral Lord Fraser of North Cape) said at Operation Trident recently their usefulness is not finished. Weight of armour and armament will still be required and battleships will also fill a vital role as platforms for guided missiles now being developed.

From 1949 to September 1954 *Vanguard*'s employment was

Below: An excellent view of the forward 15in guns and bridge. Note that the STAAG twin Bofors mount on 'B' turret was usually covered with a tarpaulin. Photo c. 1950.

Above: *Vanguard* 'all lit up' whilst at anchor during Cowes Week in 1950.

limited and low-profile. Short deployments abroad for showing the flag, children's parties on board, official and celebrity entertainment and laying at anchor with the odd Navy Day for the public became her normal role. Entering Devonport in September 1954 for a so-called refit saw her just lying in the dockyard until December 1955 which had simply been a case of buying time to consider just what to do with her in the long term. In September 1954 the Admiralty wrote:

> For both manpower and financial reasons in order to keep *Vanguard* in commission two 6in cruisers would have to be taken out of the Active Fleet and placed in Reserve. For peacetime and cold war purposes the value of having a battleship in commission is great. It is an impressive representation of naval might and unsurpassed for the training of young officers and men. On the other hand, our 6in cruisers are not unimpressive and the alternative of keeping two of these cruisers in commission instead of *Vanguard* would allow greater flexibility in meeting our peacetime commitments all over the world. Nevertheless, balancing cold war and hot war requirements, the Admiralty consider that the number of cruisers cannot be further reduced and for this reason regretfully conclude that *Vanguard* must go into Reserve.

In September 1955 it was announced that *Vanguard* was to go into Reserve but in High A Category status. A statement was issued to the Press:

> The Admiralty have decided not to commission *Vanguard* when she completes her refit in a few months' time. The value of *Vanguard* in war remains unquestioned, but for her role in such an event she can, after the periodical refit which she is being given, be kept available in Reserve at the required degree of readiness. In peacetime, however, the smaller ships which are her equivalent in manpower and which would be the price of her commissioning are collectively of greater value, especially at the present time. On completion of her current refit *Vanguard* will therefore be place in Reserve.

Her long refit had consisted of very little in the way of improvements except for the Mk 37 directors receiving an update. Modification of some internal compartments was not carried out and her dry-docking at the end of the refit was cancelled. During this period there were debates over the fitting of missiles to existing ships and *Vanguard* was one of them. The US and French navies were also studying such modifications for their cruisers and battleships. It would require the removal of one or two main

Vanguard on her way home from Gibraltar in 1951. Note the whip aerials on the bridge and forecastle.

Vanguard on her way to Gibraltar in January 1951 to carry out various exercises with other units of the Mediterranean Fleet.

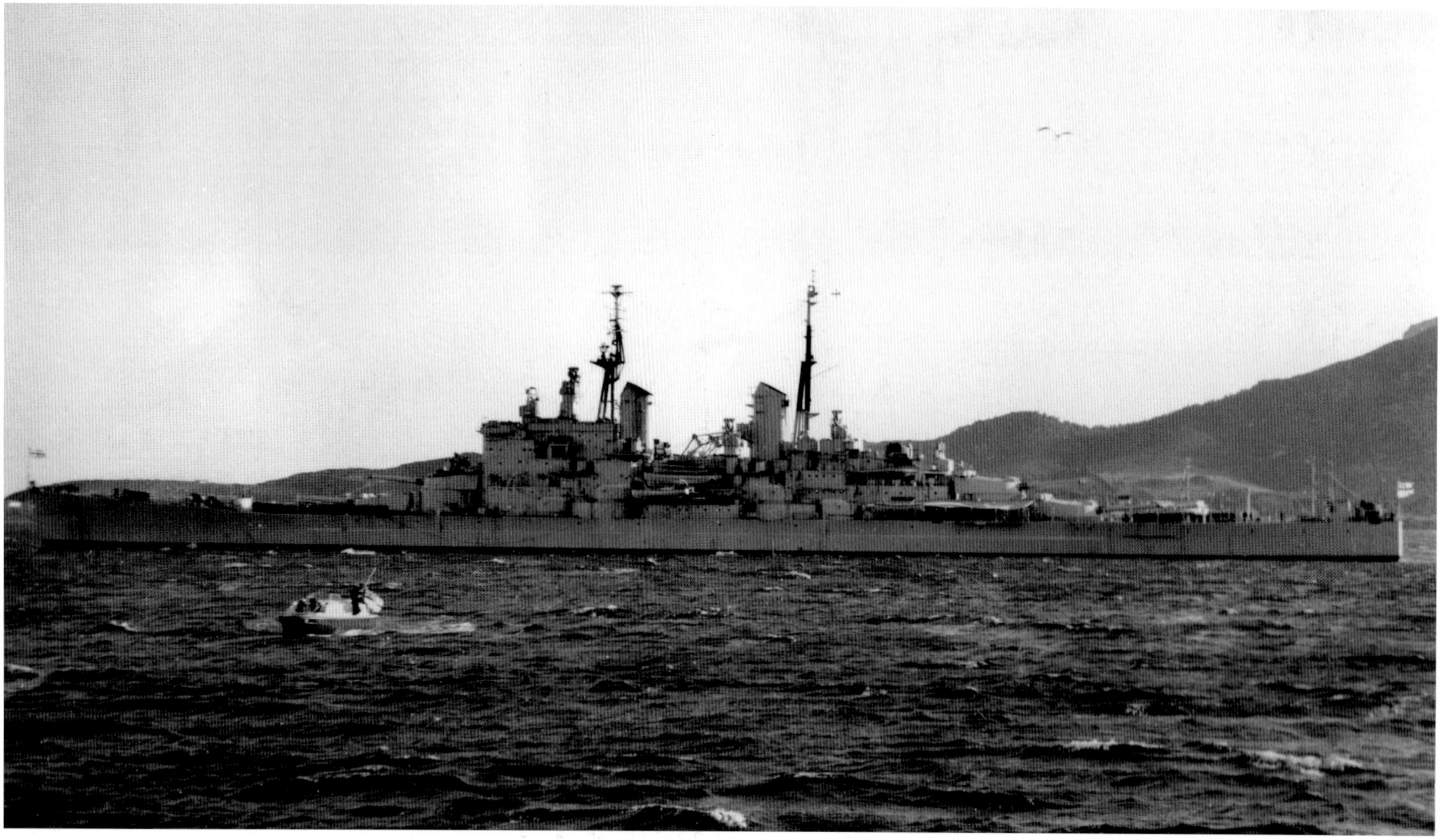

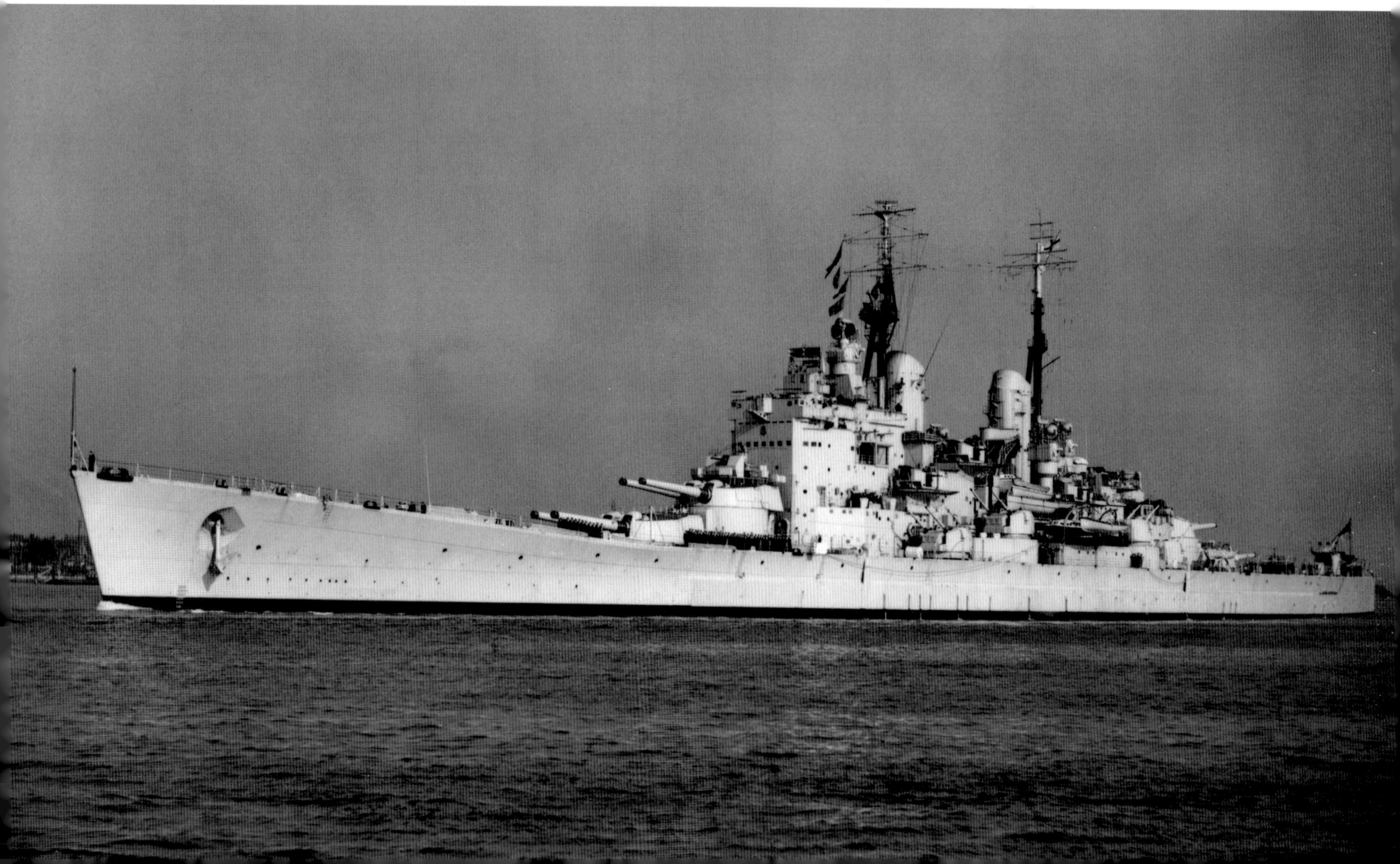

CRITICISM OF VANGUARD AND THE DEMISE OF THE BATTLESHIP

Left: On 10 February 1951 whilst the aircraft carrier *Indomitable* was berthing alongside at Gibraltar, a strong gust of wind carried her into the stern of *Vanguard* who was anchored nearby causing damage to her transom stern and creating a gash in the plating. Nothing serious but it had to be temporarily patched with concrete until the ship could be permanently repaired. Note the short ensign staff which was also damaged in the incident.

Left: A port broadside view of *Vanguard* during the 1953 Coronation Fleet Review.

Right: Close-up of *Vanguard* and the destroyer *Scorpion* fully dressed for Navy Day at Portsmouth on 4 August 1952. This event attracted 59,360 people with *Vanguard* being the biggest attraction and recording 48,173 visitors, her nearest rival being the aircraft carrier *Perseus*.

H.M.S. VANGUARD

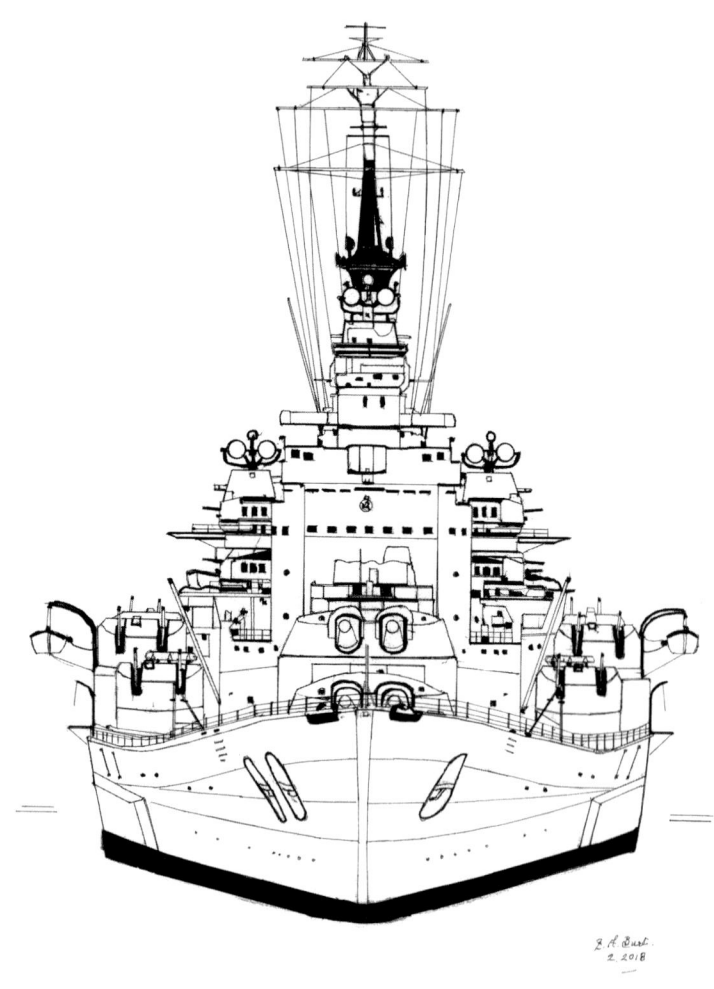

Vanguard bow-on view, 1946.
Vanguard presented a very up-to-date and heavy streamlined appearance, especially when viewed from this angle. With a beam of 108ft and her forward starfish, masts and aerials towering over the bridge structure, she presented a magnificent view that impressed all who saw her.

Vanguard, 1946.
Looking down on Vanguard's bridge (starboard side) as completed (1946) showing forward funnel, mast, 6-barrel 40mm Bofors mounts, Type 262 RDF positions and boat deck.

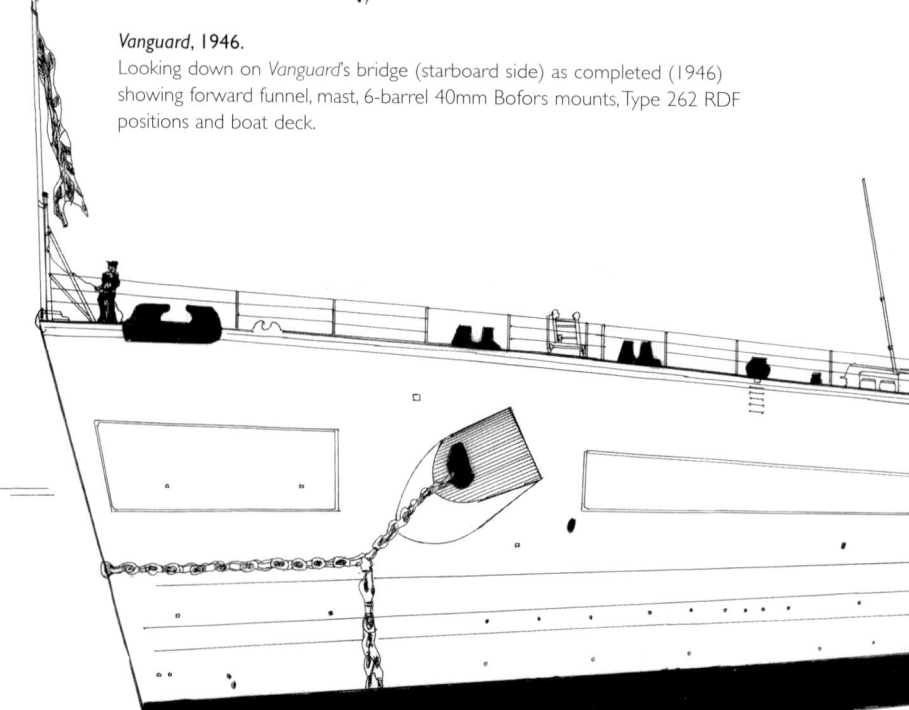

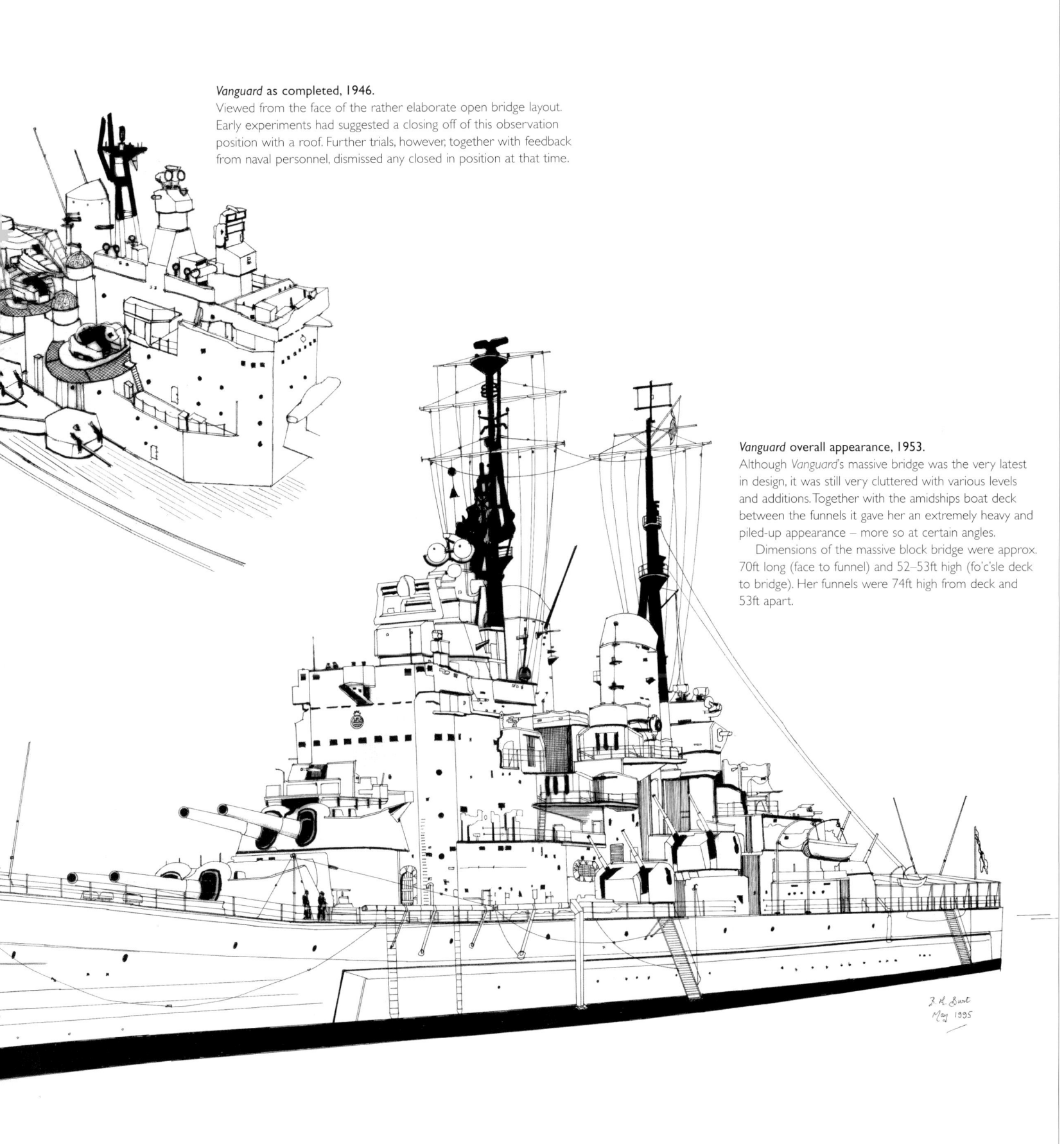

Vanguard as completed, 1946.
Viewed from the face of the rather elaborate open bridge layout. Early experiments had suggested a closing off of this observation position with a roof. Further trials, however, together with feedback from naval personnel, dismissed any closed in position at that time.

Vanguard overall appearance, 1953.
Although *Vanguard*'s massive bridge was the very latest in design, it was still very cluttered with various levels and additions. Together with the amidships boat deck between the funnels it gave her an extremely heavy and piled-up appearance – more so at certain angles.

Dimensions of the massive block bridge were approx. 70ft long (face to funnel) and 52–53ft high (fo'c'sle deck to bridge). Her funnels were 74ft high from deck and 53ft apart.

turrets which would be replaced with a suitable missile platform. Although this was given considerable thought it was not, however, put into practice, certainly with the battleships, the main reasons being the cost, the long period of reconstruction, complications with stability and in general, changing the role for which the ship was built. It seemed much easier to fit missiles to ships of cruiser size which was not only more practical but more cost-effective and any suggestion of *Vanguard* receiving such changes was dropped. (Some of the *Iowa* class battleships were fitted with missiles during the 1980s but no main gun turrets were removed.)

Vanguard left Devonport in December 1955 but the preparation for her entrance into the Reserve was underway. In Category A status she was to be ready for steaming at 20 knots on 30 days' notice and the main and secondary armament ready for action in three months but the close-range AA armament was to be removed. *Vanguard* was then moored alongside HMS *Howe* in the Hamoaze.

From 1956 to 1958 *Vanguard* declined. Now being used as a training ship with the status of Flagship of the Reserve Fleet she did very little in the way of serious naval activity. She finally left Devonport in October 1956 and returned to Portsmouth whereupon she became a training ship and accommodation ship with many of her spaces being used for offices and cadet training. In 1958 her status was reduced to Category C. It now became just a matter of time for the Admiralty and Government to work out how to dispose of her in the most suitable way and in August 1959 a Board Committee issued the following memorandum to all concerned:

Following the directive by the Board on M287/6/58 'The Way Ahead' we have considered the ways in which HMS *Vanguard* could be relieved of her present functions so that she may be disposed of without delay. In carrying out this examination it has been borne in mind that there is considerable political interest in the future of *Vanguard* and that the Select Committee on estimates have recommended that 'if no positive function can be found for HMS *Vanguard* she should be disposed of'. HMS *Vanguard* is for all practical purposes in Extended Reserve although she is shown in the Pink List, mainly for customs purposes, as in Supplementary Reserve. She is the accommodation ship for Flag Officer Commanding Reserve Fleet and his staff and for the Portsmouth Division of the Reserve Fleet. In addition certain training functions are carried out on board. The cost of maintaining her in 1957/8

Below: Port quarter view as *Vanguard* nears Portsmouth, May 1953.

Opposite, bottom: Superb view of *Vanguard* on 1 June 1953 shortly after the Coronation Fleet Review.

CRITICISM OF VANGUARD AND THE DEMISE OF THE BATTLESHIP

Vanguard in the Spithead Roads for the Coronation Fleet Review, May 1953. Seen from the air fully dressed for the Royal Inspection. On the day before the review the public had slowly but steadily been arriving in the Portsmouth and Southsea area. Estimates at the time by the AA gave figures of over 20,000 cars coming into the area and up to 1,000,000 people expected to squeeze into every available space to witness the Review. Thousands of people were known to have slept on the beach and surrounding areas to get a good position on the day of the review. The Queen and Duke of Edinburgh inspected the Fleet from HMS *Surprise* which had been fitted with a special viewing platform for them owing to the fact that the new Royal Yacht *Britannia* had not been ready in time. They inspected the Fleet for over 1½ hours before HMS *Surprise* anchored off the port quarter of *Vanguard*. On the evening after the review on 15 May the Royal party dined with Sir George Creasy the CinC of the Home Fleet in the wardroom of *Vanguard*.

Left: Public Navy Days were always immensely popular and when *Vanguard* was available to visit the dockyard was extremely busy. The visits to the ship in 1952 and 1953 saw thousands crawling over every inch of the ship (where permitted) and the photograph shows this as an eager public pace themselves up to the top of her forecastle.

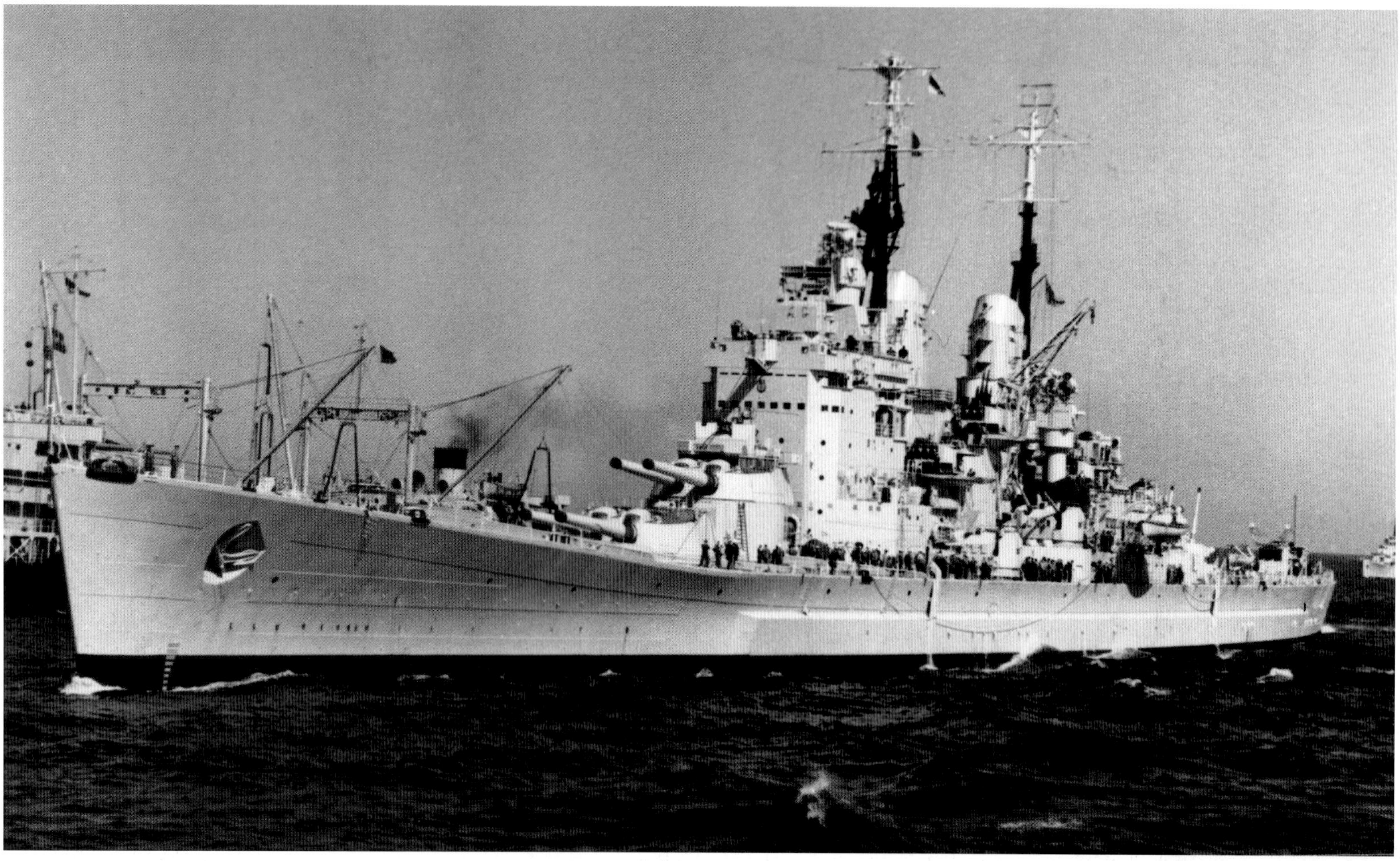

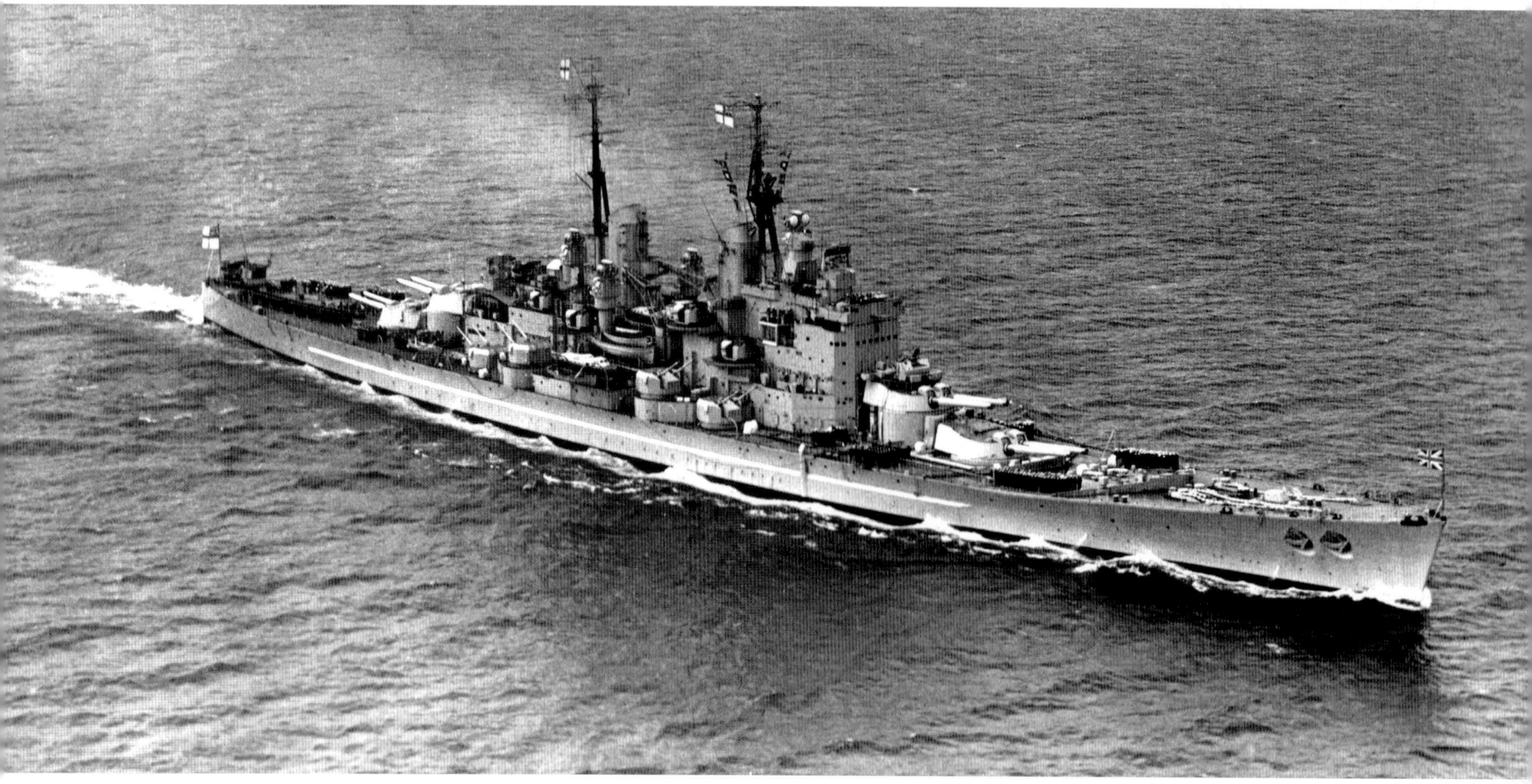

has been publicly announced as £230,000 which included £150,000 for the cost of the Category crew.

There followed a long debate on how to carefully remove her from the effective list and whilst this was going on there was some intimation of a sale to Chile but nothing came of this with both sides not too eager on such a move. When the news of the disposal was circulated within the Admiralty it was met with a mixture of relief and despair. Most were relieved for obvious reasons but there were also many in despair at the passing of the Royal Navy's last battleship and it was this group that made their voices heard in no uncertain terms. The First Sea Lord, Admiral Sir Frederick Parham, was one these and although he accepted that there was no suitable active role for *Vanguard*, he pleaded for her to be preserved as some sort of museum ship. He believed that thousands would constantly flock to see her in Devonport as they did to Portsmouth to see HMS *Victory*. He asked if someone could estimate on how much this would cost. Having just read an article in the *National and English Review* about *Vanguard* he was so taken by it that he sent a copy to the DNC on 17 October 1959:

> Trafalgar Day finds only two battleships at Portsmouth – the *Victory* and the *Vanguard*. The *Victory*, whose masts and yards preside over the dockyard, is safely berthed ashore; the *Vanguard* tied up alongside is destined for the scrap heap. The ninth of her name, she is the last of an immensely long and honourable line. No more battleships will ever be built. For the first time in a thousand years navies no longer demand the largest warships of which designers and shipyards are capable. The *Vanguard* marks not the end of an era but the end of a whole series of eras. She is also the final achievement of a nation whose contribution to history has been based on sea power. Should she be destroyed? It is true we carry a sufficient burden of preservation already but the *Vanguard* is different from a country house. If one country house is preserved a cry goes up to save ten others; if one country house falls down many more will survive. But *Vanguard* is unique. Moreover, with the possible exception of HMS *Hood*, she is the finest capital ship we have ever produced.

But on 31 December 1959 the DNC gave the expected answer:

> My Dear Freddie,
> I am sorry that it has taken me so long to send you a full reply to your letter of 17th October, about *Vanguard*, but at this time of the year it is difficult. The preliminary costing of your idea for preserving *Vanguard* has now been completed and I am afraid the result is as prophesised in my note of 19th October. In a nutshell, it would cost just about as much money and manpower to maintain the *Vanguard* to the standards expected of a national showpiece as it has to keep her in operational Reserve. She is as you know, the object of pretty lively political interest and the First Lord and the Civil Lord would have a hard time defending this kind of expenditure in Parliament. Apart from the question of resources, although I entirely share your regret at the approaching demise of so lovely a ship as the *Vanguard*, I and many others feel that the comparison between her and the *Victory* does not really stand up to even the most sympathetic examination. There is no getting away from the fact that this *Vanguard* never fired a shot in anger, is something less than the ideal symbol of naval achievement. Our detractors may be relatively few but they do exist

Opposite, top: *Vanguard* is shown here during exercises in 1953 and is carrying out refuelling practice before joining other ships of the Fleet including NATO vessels for Operation 'Mariner' which included the American battleship *Iowa*.

Opposite, bottom: *Vanguard* on 14 May 1954 on her way to rendezvous with HMS *Triumph*, *Glasgow* and two destroyers which then met the Royal Yacht *Britannia* on her way back from HM The Queen and Duke of Edinburgh's Commonwealth tour. Units of the Home Fleet led by *Vanguard* fired a salute and then took up position astern of *Britannia*. Admiral Sir Michael Denny on board *Vanguard* passed a message to the Queen 'It is with intense pride that we your Majesty's Home Fleet escort you into your United Kingdom'

Above: Close-up of *Vanguard* in March 1954 giving a clear view of her 5.25in turrets and Type 274 and 275 radars, as well as her six barrel 40mm Bofors mounts.

and on occasion they are pretty vociferous. Setting the *Vanguard* alongside the *Victory* might give them a field day.

Following this a request was issued arrangements to be made for towing the *Vanguard* away to the breakers as soon as possible after June 1960 when she would be relieved as Reserve Fleet Headquarters by two smaller ships. Her de-equipping and removal of any valuable items was to start immediately.

When this news became know there were a variety of responses but most were rather sympathetic to the decisions. *The Navy* gave its thoughts:

So *Vanguard* after a series of sentences and reprieves is finally to go to the ship-breakers. It is very sad that so powerful and so beautiful a warship should come to the end of her life. Yet it may be, and we are in no position to judge, that her

Right: Bow photograph of *Vanguard* showing her fine lines as she anchors in Torbay, May 1954.

Opposite, top: *Vanguard* off Berry Head on 8 May 1954 preparing to meet the Royal Yacht *Britannia*.

Opposite, bottom: *Vanguard* flying the Flag of CinC of Home Fleet Sir Michael Denny and dressed overall for the departure of the Royal Yacht *Britannia*. Seen alongside the South Railway Jetty on 14 April 1954.

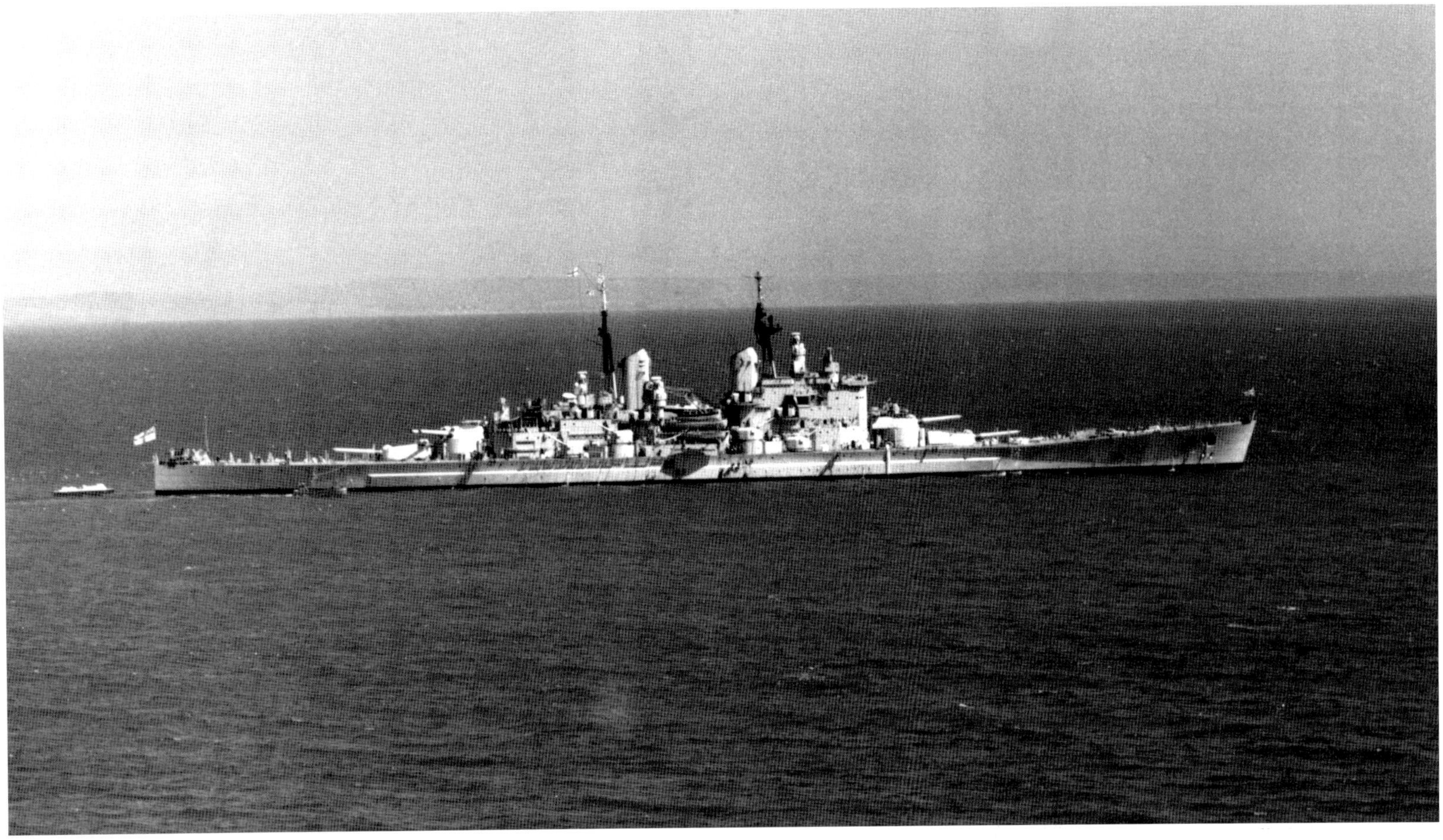

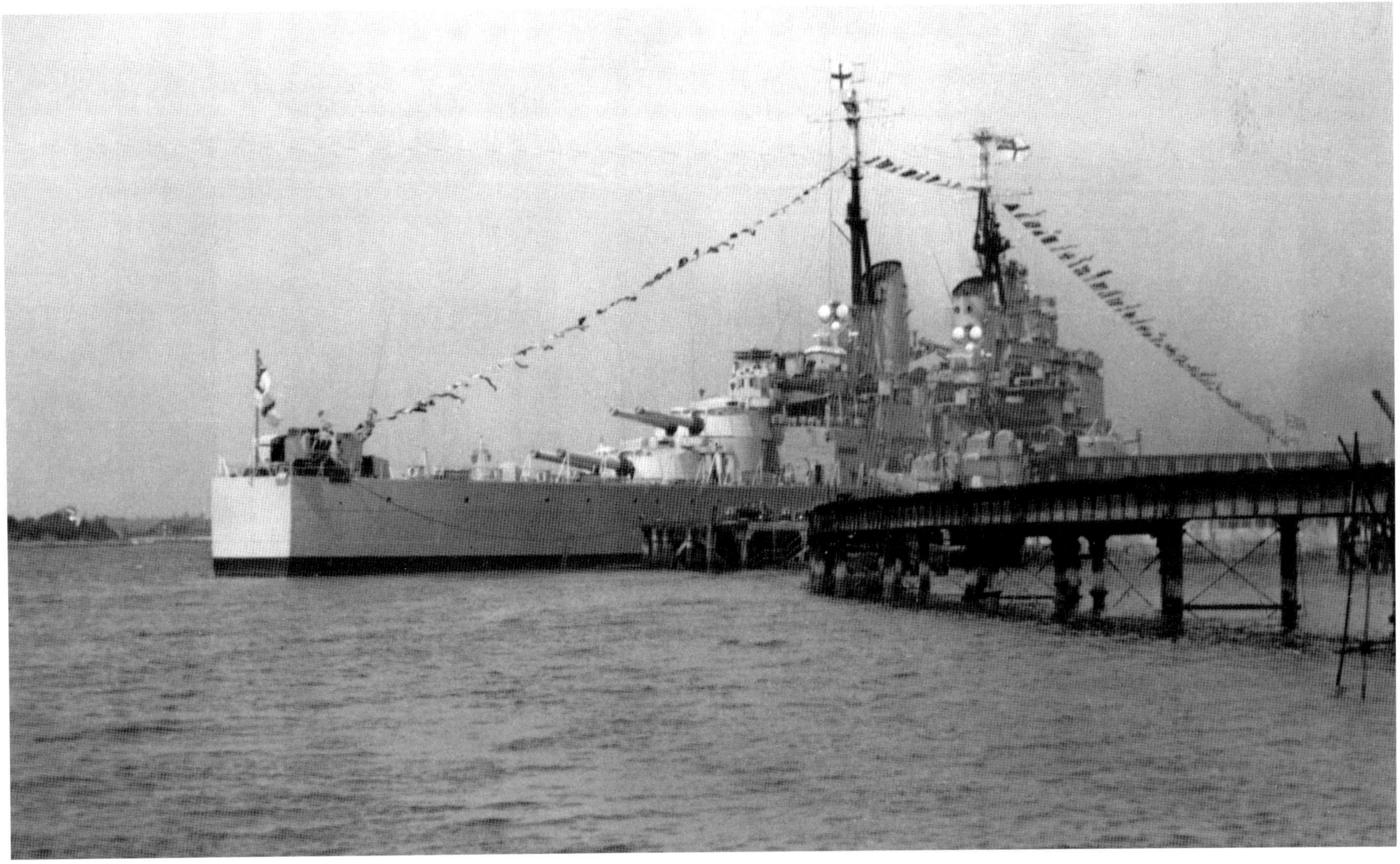

Above: The beginning of the end, 1956. *Vanguard* is moored up alongside HMS *Howe* after she was relegated to the Reserve Fleet. Note that *Howe* has been mothballed already and the six-barrel 40mm Bofors mounts on *Vanguard* are being stripped and removed.

retention cannot be justified in so rapidly changing naval scene at so larger cost, both of men and money.

Vanguard paid off to the Disposal list on 7 June 1960 on the same day as this article appeared in the *Birmingham Post*:

Britain's remaining battleship will be de-commissioned this evening. When the colours of HMS *Vanguard*, Britain's only remaining battleship, are hauled down this evening it will be the end of an era for the Royal Navy. For the *Vanguard* will sail no more under the White Ensign and no more battleships will be built. Revolutionary changes in the pattern of warfare have brought about the demise of the battleship, once the grim steel grey symbol of Britain's might. Those of us who attended Fleet reviews remember how fine the show of battleships and battlecruisers made steaming in line ahead, the epitome of naval power. And how the names rolled off the tongue – *Royal Sovereign, Resolution, Ramillies, Revenge, Barham, Malaya* and

Warspite. We know now that the confidence placed in the battleships was mistaken. The passing of the *Vanguard* signifying as it does the end of the 'battle wagon' will have brought lumps to the throats of many old sailors and the ceremony of hauling down the Ensign will symbolise more than an ordinary sunset. For the battleship there will be no dawn.

HMS *Vanguard* was finally towed out of Portsmouth on 4 August 1960 bound for the Faslane and the scrapyard. She had been in service for just fourteen years, about the same time as the first of her type, HMS *Dreadnought* of 1906. One of the first items to get chopped off with the cutter's acetylene torch were her 15in guns, the very items which were the genesis of her conception.

And so *Vanguard* passed into history, the last of her kind to serve in the Royal Navy. A history which encompassed the wooden ship of the line, the ironclad, the pre-dreadnought, the dreadnought and the super-dreadnought – a type of ship that had served Great Britain so well for hundreds of years had finally ceased to exist.

Above: Stern view of *Vanguard* and *Howe* as above and moored in the Hamoaze, 1956.

Appendix A: Service History

The name *Vanguard* had originally been chosen for a proposed fifth unit of the *Lion* class of 1938.
Ordered from John Brown on 14 March 1941. Laid down at Clydebank on 2 October 1941.
Her construction prior to launch was extremely slow but was then accelerated with a view to her taking part in operations against the Japanese fleet in the Pacific.
Launched on St Andrews Day, 30 November 1944.
Whilst fitting out in September 1945, there was a small explosion on board, probably a gas bottle, and two men were killed.
Commissioned at Clydebank for early trials on 25 April 1946.
Early trials period May 1946. Gunnery trials off the coast of Ireland, steam trials following in June–July.
Final acceptance trials 8 August 1946. Accepted on 9 August but was still to undergo more extensive trials. Further trials were carried out and recorded by Captain W G Agnew as follows:

HMS *Vanguard* slipped from Middle Slip Jetty, His Majesty's Dockyard, Portsmouth at 0715 on Wednesday 4th December 1946.

With a wind West North Force 4 the ship turned with the aid of tugs and left harbour without incident and anchored in St Helens Bay at 08.30. During the afternoon the ship calibrated her DF and radar.

At 13.40 hours *Vanguard* weighed anchor and proceeded down Channel with HMS *Obedient* in company for W/T tests.

At 03.15 on Thursday 5th December course was set for Madeira. The ship passed through the Madeira Islands on Saturday 7th December and proceeded to the south westward in order to ensure good weather for various exercises it was desired to carry out. She passed the Canary Islands on Tuesday 10th December and thence to Gibraltar. Throughout the cruise from Portsmouth to Gibraltar opportunity was taken to test the new Radio equipment which had been fitted for the Royal tour, side screen and awning curtains, sending away sea boats, man ship, various gunnery and damage control drills and generally getting the officers and men settled down to sea routine. Fuel consumption trials at various speeds, with 4 and 2 shafts and 8 and 4 boilers were also carried out.

Vanguard passed through the Straits of Gibraltar at 07.00 on Friday 13th December and carried out radar trials with HMS *Chivalrous* and aircraft to the eastward, later entering Gibraltar harbour at 14.30 hours and securing at the South Mole. The ship was open to visitors from 14.00 to 17.00 on Saturday 14th December.

Vanguard slipped from the South Mole at 10.00 hours on Monday 16th December and made a sternboard out through the Southern entrance. Whilst passing through Straits of Gibraltar the transference of mails by jackstay methods was exercised with HMS *Chivalrous* and gunnery tracking exercises were carried out with her and an aircraft. During passage to Portsmouth further fuel consumption trials with 8 and 4 boilers were carried out.

On Thursday 19th December trials of oiling at sea by the astern method with Royal Fleet Auxiliary *Brown Ranger* was carried out. At 15.00 hours the tow was cast off and *Vanguard* proceeded towards the Nab Tower with the visibility reduced to a mile. When in estimated position 3 miles East South East of the Nab, three buoys flashing quickly were sighted. These could not be found on the chart and as no fix had been obtained for a long time and nothing could be seen or heard

Right: Close-up of *Howe* and *Vanguard* in the Hamoaze, 1956.

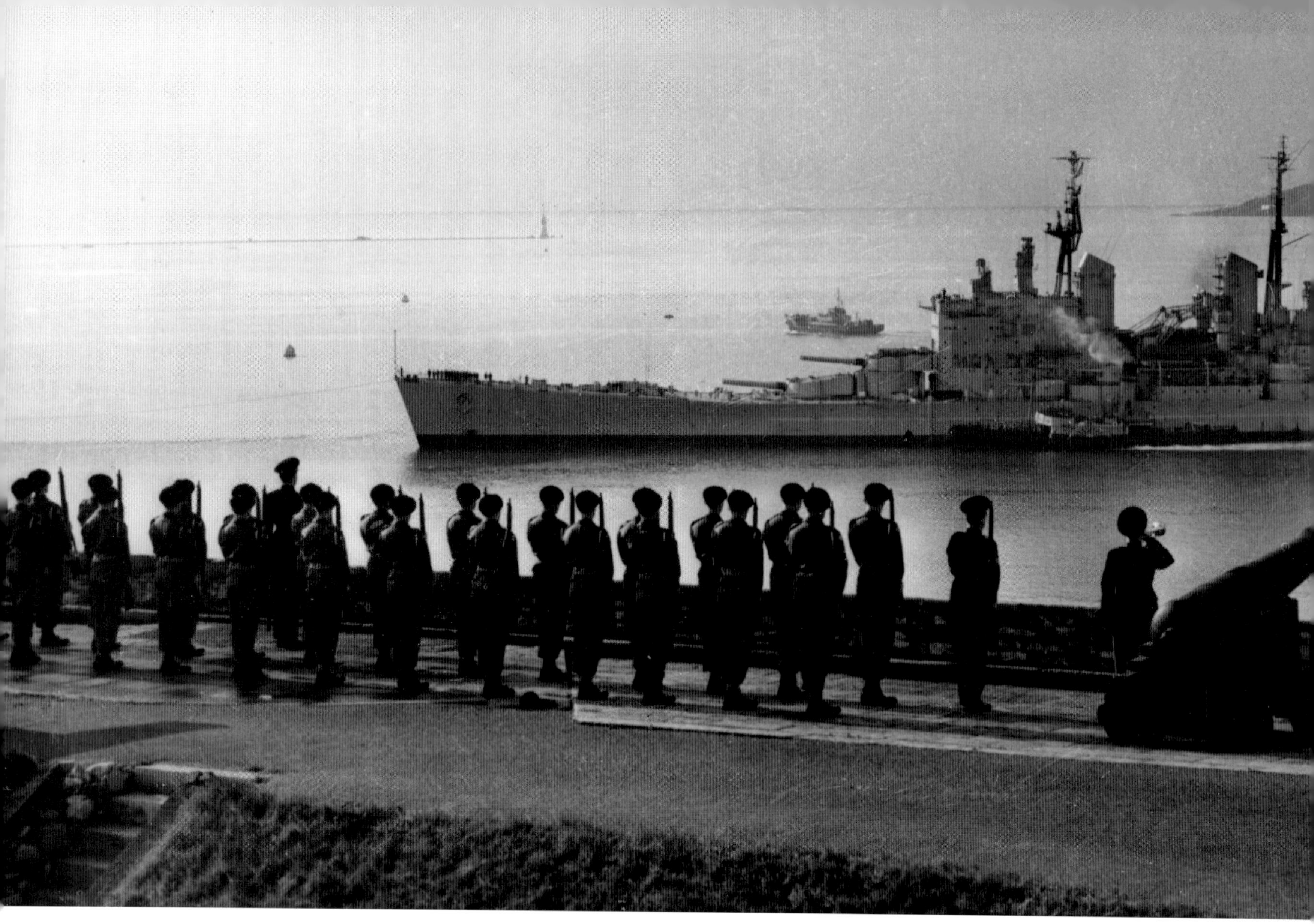

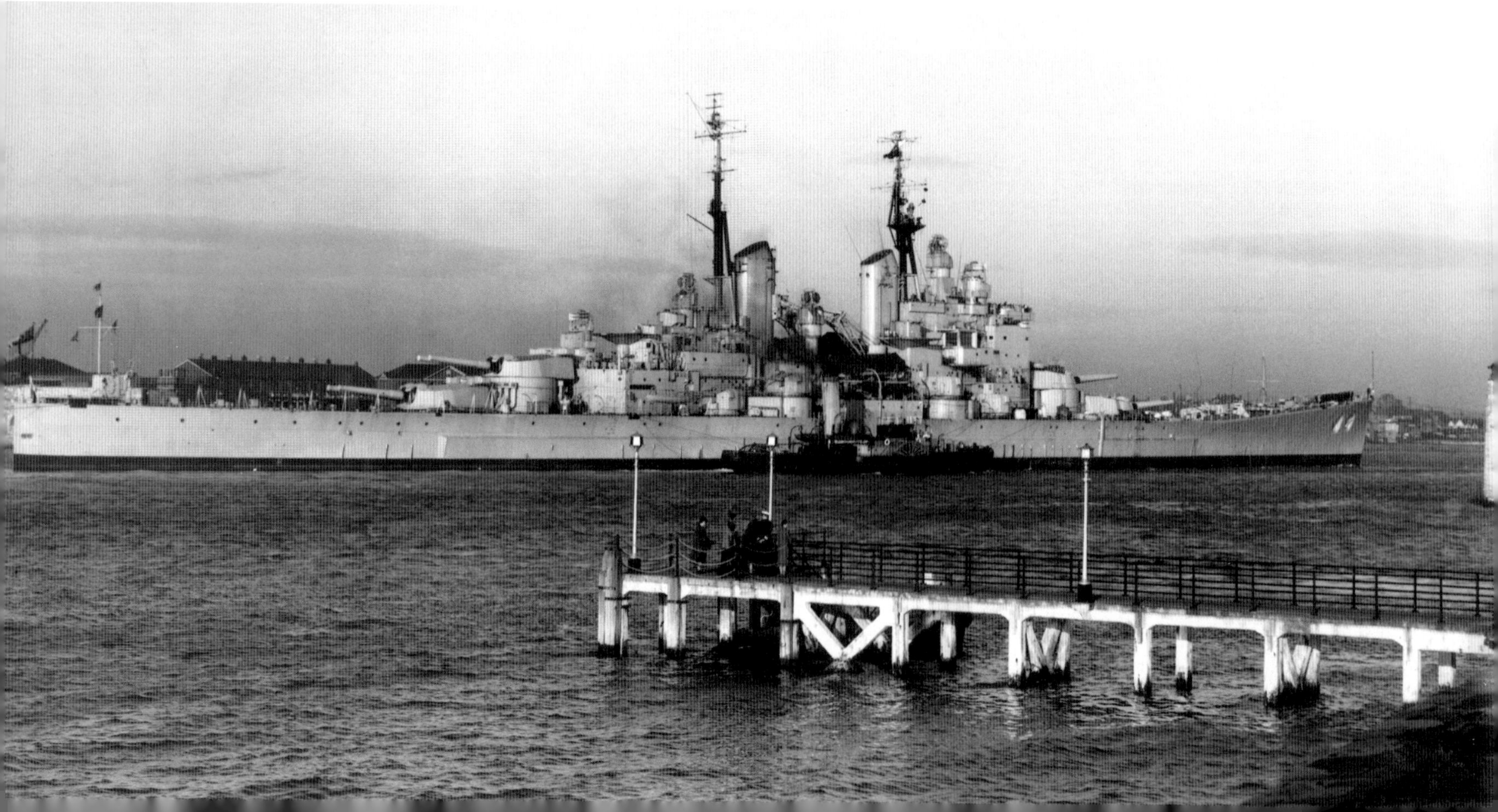

Left: Looking across to *Vanguard* as she leaves Plymouth for the last time on 26 October 1956 the guard of honour from the 47th Light Anti-Aircraft Regiment RA (formerly 47th Coast Regiment RA) present arms in a salute to the ship as she is towed downstream.

Below, left: *Vanguard* being towed toward Portsmouth Dockyard watched by a few bystanders in October 1956.

Below: Superstructure of *Vanguard*. Compare this view with that of March 1954 to note the changes of her demise.

of the Nab, the ship was anchored in spite of what appeared to be a good plot on the radar type 293 PPI. An hour and a half later the visibility improved and the Nab Tower light was sighted. The ship weighed and proceeded anchoring at Spithead at 20.30 hours.

Vanguard entered Portsmouth Harbour at 09.30 on Friday 20th December and secured at the South Railway Jetty.

As shown in the report above, the trials of *Vanguard* were extensive and ongoing during her run-up to the Royal Tour.

Portsmouth, August 1946 to February 1947. Refitting for Royal Tour during last months of 1946 (accommodation areas, removal of some 40mm Bofors and radar aerial on main topmast removed for the Flying of the Royal Standard).

Modifications were completed by the end of January 1947.

Royal Tour. South Africa. February to May 1947.

Left Portsmouth for Cape Town 1 February.

Escorted down the Channel by HMS *Implacable*, *Diadem*, *Cleopatra* and *St James*.

Returned to Portsmouth on 11 May 1947 and placed in Reserve at Devonport for small refit to reassemble altered equipment back into naval use. June 1947 to February 1948.

Reserve. Devonport. June 1947 to September 1948.

Selected in March 1948 to take the King and Queen and Princess Margaret on a proposed visit to Australia and New Zealand in the spring of 1948 but this was later cancelled owing to the poor health of the King.

She was sent to the Mediterranean for special exercises in September 1948.

Mediterranean, September 1948 to November 1948.

Vanguard's forecastle during preparations to tow the ship to Faslane, June 1960.

Carried out extensive exercises from Malta.
Returned to Devonport on 12 November 1948.
Devonport. Reserve, November 1948 to January 1949.
Transferred to the Mediterranean January 1949.
Mediterranean, January to July 1949. Five-day visit to Naples 29 March 1949.
Refit at Devonport from July to November 1949. Relieved HMS *Victorious* as Flagship of the Home Fleet, Portland 1 November 1949.
Home Fleet, November 1949 to September 1954. Flag Training Squadron to May 1952. Fleet Flag later.
Temporary Fleet Flag for exercises during autumn 1950 and spring 1951. Refit at Devonport October 1951 to February 1952. Five-day visit to Genoa February 1951.
Replaced HMS *Indomitable* as Fleet Flag in May 1952 owing to inadequate staff accommodation in the carrier.
Took part in the NATO Exercise 'Mainbrace' in the Arctic and North Sea 13–25 September 1952, the largest exercise of its kind held to that date.
Fleet flagship at Spithead for Coronation Review 15 May 1953.
Took part in the NATO Exercise 'Mariner' in the Atlantic, North Sea and Channel 16 September to 5 October 1953. Visit to Halsingborg, Sweden, on a one-week goodwill visit.
Relieved as Flagship by the destroyer depot ship *Tyne* and paid off at Devonport for refit in September 1954.
Refit at Devonport from September 1954 to December 1955.
Originally to have recommissioned for further service in Home Fleet after refit but she was reduced to high-category reserve at Devonport instead. Part of her crew were appropriated to assisting the guided missile trials ship *Girdle Ness* and some smaller ships.
Reserve December 1955 to June 1960. Devonport to October 1956, Portsmouth later. Flagship of Reserve Fleet at Portsmouth 28 November 1956.
Employed as Training, Accommodation and Reserve Fleet Headquarters ship.
Maintained in high state operational reserve from 1956 to 1958 and allocated for use to NATO if required.
Reduced to lower status of reserve late in 1958 as it was stated in Parliament in July of that year that NATO obligations requiring high-state readiness had terminated.
Paid off to the disposal list at Portsmouth 7 June 1960.
Sold to Shipbreaking Industries Ltd, Faslane June 1960 for an alleged sum of £550,000.
Left Portsmouth in tow on 4 August 1960 for Faslane to be scrapped.
Arrived at Faslane on 9 August.

H.M.S. VANGUARD	
1586	1960
THE ARMADA 1588	LOWESTOFT 1665
CADIZ 1596	FOUR DAYS BATTLE 1666
THE KENTISH KNOCK 1652	St JAMES' DAY 1666
DUNGENESS 1652	BARFLEUR 1692
PORTLAND 1653	QUEBEC 1759
THE GABBARD 1653	THE NILE 1798
THE TEXEL 1653	JUTLAND 1916

Above: HMS *Vanguard* gets the final farewell salute from Marine bugler Ian Davies as her flag is lowered for the last time on 7 June 1960. On 27 July 1960 a rather blunt report about *Vanguard* appeared in the *Daily Telegraph*: 'Britain's last battleship, the 44,500 ton *Vanguard* with 8 x 15in and smaller guns cost about £11,000,000 when completed 14 years ago is to be towed from Portsmouth on August 4th for her last voyage to the breakers yard at Faslane on the Clyde. The White Elephant Ship which has never fired her guns in anger belongs to the navies of yesterday. With post war developments and the advance of ships of the "new" navies of the atomic age, there is no place in the fleet for a battleship.'

Left: Quarterdeck during preparations to tow the ship to Faslane, June 1960.

Above: Stern of *Vanguard* as she is prepared for towing, 4 August 1960.

Left: As *Vanguard* left Portsmouth for the last time under tow on 4 August 1960 she strayed to port and ran aground near Old Sally Port, causing much excitement amongst the crowd nearby. As seen her bow is close to the Customs House Hailing Point and her port anchor was dropped to stop the vessel going any further. Finally freed by desperate tugs after much anxiety all around, she was pulled out of Portsmouth to begin her journey to the scrap yard.

Right: After a very slow final journey *Vanguard* arrives at Faslane on 9 August 1960.

APPENDIX A: SERVICE HISTORY

Above: Looking up at 'X' 15in gun turret and aft superstructure. Note that the turret plates have been numbered for removal in sections. September 1960.

Right: An internal view of one of her 15in gun turrets showing the complex breech mechanism. Note how cramped it is with the gun cradles taking up most of the space.

APPENDIX A: SERVICE HISTORY 121

Above: *Vanguard*'s quarterdeck photographed on 11 August 1960 shortly after berthing in the scrapyard.

Above: *Vanguard*'s quarterdeck on 3 September 1960, photographed just a few weeks after the image above. Already her 15in guns have gone and her turret tops have been cut through and removed; parts of the after superstructure as well as the DCT have been taken away.

Above: The severed 15in guns being craned from the ship, September 1960.

Right: Many of the smaller fittings on the upper deck have been removed as well as the 15in guns and best part of the turrets. The photo shows a worker from Shipbreaking Industries.

APPENDIX A: SERVICE HISTORY

These workers were called burners and used heavy-duty oxy-propane torches of the Glasgow type for most of the work. November 1960.

Right: Bow-on and undergoing disposal with a worker slicing through the 15in gun sections in the foreground. These guns were the first items to be severed from the ship after *Vanguard* was secured alongside at Faslane. Taken during September–November 1960.

Above: The remains of the hull seen on an overcast and cold day but still being of interest and filmed as well as photographed to the very end. 1961.

Left: The last section of *Vanguard*'s bow as it lies in the mud, 2 April 1962.

Appendix B: Comparison with the French *Jean Bart* and the US *Iowa*

It is a popular pastime amongst battleship cognoscenti to compare ships of the Royal Navy with contemporaries from foreign powers. None more so than the capital ships of the final generation around the time of the Second World War – *Tirpitz*, *Iowa*, *Littorio*, *Jean Bart/Richelieu* and of course the giant *Yamato*. Questions and suggestions are put forward to analyse who would be the winner in a classic face-to-face confrontation – disregarding of course any aircraft attacks. The scenarios discussed are often quite detailed, and at times rather heated. There are reams of correspondence that have been written and debated over the years depicting such actions, but the result it seems, ends in ever-turning circles. There is no definite conclusion. The assumption of a winner during a sea duel is only on paper and is in the mind of individuals based on the way they see the course of the action. We often do not agree with each other. Even official reports are only an educated and calculated opinion judged on the statistics of any particular vessel placed before them.

By the time *Vanguard* was completed the enemy battleships had been sunk in one way or another, although it was never doubted that the German *Tirpitz*, the Italian *Littorio* and indeed the Japanese *Yamato* would have been formidable foes. This just leaves a comparison with ships of the Allied navies – *Iowa* and *Jean Bart/Richelieu* – but it has to be repeated that it is still only on paper that comparison can be drawn. The French *Jean Bart* was very similar to *Vanguard* in being a post-war battleship that had benefited from war experience in her design and both had also been delayed in their construction, finally completing after hostilities had ended. If documents are to be believed, then neither of these two ships was actually wanted by their respective governments. *Iowa*, *Jean Bart* and *Vanguard* were all excellent ships and on par with each other. Of course one can say that one vessel has an extra 1in or 2in of armour and an extra 1in on the gun calibre and perhaps a knot or two faster than the other, having more efficient machinery, but in reality no source can claim who would be the victor in a pure surface action with so much to be considered – weather conditions, ship fully worked-up, an efficient regular crew who have trained constantly with the equipment available to them, tactics, command and control of the ship by experienced officers, and of course, that very important factor – luck – who hits who first and where those hits strike the target.

PARTICULARS OF *JEAN BART* AND *IOWA*

	Jean Bart	Iowa
Displacement:	48,950 tons	56,000 tons
Length:	813ft	887ft
Beam:	116ft over bulge	108ft
Draught:	30/32ft	33ft
Main armament:	8 × 15in	9 × 16in
Secondary armament:	9 × 6in	20 × 5in
	24 × 3.9in DP	19 × 4-barrel 40mm
	28 × 57mm AA	52 × 20mm
Armour		
Main belt	15–7in	12in
Decks	6–7in	5–6in
Turrets	17–7in	17–2in
Barbettes	16–4in	17–1in
CT	13½in	17in
Machinery:	150,000 shp	212,000 shp (design)
Fuel:	5,800 tons oil	7,800 tons oil
Speed:	30/32 knots	31/32 knots
Radius of action:	8,250 miles @ 20 knots	11,700 miles @ 20 knots
Complement:	1,280	1,800

All too often British battleships are slated for their faults and of course they had them, but so did those of all other navies: in fact, there was never a battleship built worldwide that did not have weak areas and could be considered perfect. *Vanguard* was a good match for any comparable battleship in the period in which she was built.

For completeness, it will suffice to list the two ships' statistics that can be compared to *Vanguard* and leave it up to the reader to form his own opinion, and of course give further interesting debate on a subject that will never reach a conclusion.

Regarding HMS *Vanguard* in general, although some things were wanting in the design in certain areas, she was an excellent ship and compared well with any foreign unit on a one-to-one basis. She was certainly the best battleship the Royal Navy ever had.

Bibliography

Unpublished Sources

National Maritime Museum, Greenwich
Ship's Cover.
The Design and Construction of British Warships (Caird Library).

National Archives.
Admiralty ADM papers consulted:

Ship's Book.
Ships Log.
Handbook for 15in Mk 1N gun.
Handbook for 5.25in Mk 1 gun.
Handbook for STAAG 40mm gun.
Handbook for 40mm single gun.
Battleship sketch designs.
Bridge tests and airflow.
Security at launch.
Manoeuvring and circle trials.
Armament in foreign ships.
Spring Cruise 1953.
Royal Tour to South Africa 1947.
Vibration on propellers.
Steam trials.
Steam trials and observations.
Vanguard proceedings.
Questions on battleships.
Battleships in Reserve.
Expenditure of *Vanguard*.
Whip aerial handbook.
Trials in Type 274 radar.
Admiralty steam plants.
Reconstruction Committee.
Obsolete warships.
Post-war Capital ship construction.
Remarks on Design X Capital ships.
Ship Design Policy.
Lion Class Legend of Particulars.
Fire Control.
Admiralty Radar book.
16in gun production 1945.
Battleships left in Service.
Conversion to aircraft carrier.
Japan. Influence on designs.
Vanguard protection.
Employment of battleships.
1940 class battleships.
Radar trials.
Mk 37 Directors.

Periodicals and Newspapers

Birmingham Daily Gazette.
Birmingham Post.
Daily Mail.
Daily Sketch.
Daily Telegraph.
Hampshire Telegraph.
Illustrated London News.
The Navy.
The Times.

Published Sources

Brassey's Naval Annuals, 1946 to 1960.
Friedman, Norman, *The British Battleship 1906-1946* (Seaforth Publishing, 2015).
————, *US Battleships: An Illustrated Design History* (Arms and Armour Press, 1986).
Garzke, William H, and Dulin, Robert O, *Battleships: Allied Battleships in World War II* (Naval Institute Press, 1990).
HMS Vanguard (Pamphlet published in 1947 and sold on board).
HMS Vanguard and the Royal Voyage to South Africa (1946).
Jane's Fighting Ships, 1947 to 1960.
Johnston, I, and Buxton, I, *The Battleship Builders: Constructing and Arming British Capital Ships* (Seaforth Publishing, 2013).
Jordan, John, and Dumas, Robert, *French Battleships 1922-1956* (Seaforth Publishing, 2009).
Kemp, P K, *Nine Vanguards* (Hutchinson & Co, 1951).
McCart, Neil, *HMS Vanguard 1944-1960: Britain's Last Battleship* (Maritime Books, 2001).
Morrah, Dermot, *The Royal Family in Africa* (Hutchinson, 1947).
Parkes, Oscar, *British Battleships: Warrior 1860 to Vanguard 1950: a history of design, construction and armament* (Seeley Service, 1958).
Raven, A, and Roberts, J, *Battleships of World War II* (Arms and Armour Press, 1986).

Drawings are based on Admiralty 'as fitted' plans now held at the National Maritime Museum and Admiralty Handbooks at the Imperial War Museum and National Archives. Photographs are from the author's collection.